DEPRESSED PEOPLE MAKE ME SLEEPY

DEPRESSED PEOPLE MAKE ME SLEEPY

MY CURRICULUM VITAE

M. J. Rex

authorHOUSE®

AuthorHouse™
1663 Liberty Drive
Bloomington, IN 47403
www.authorhouse.com
Phone: 1 (800) 839-8640

Published by AuthorHouse 07/09/2015

ISBN: 978-1-5049-0389-9 (sc)
ISBN: 978-1-5049-1962-3 (e)

Library of Congress Control Number: 2015910244

Contents

"The scariest thing I have ever had to do was ask a hopeless person to trust me and an invisible system that I represent when at that very same moment my own life was falling apart, I was unsure of who I was and where I belonged, and I was finding it hard to trust myself. But this is often the reality of psychology and right now this is my life." M. J. Rex

Kimberly K., Mrs. Arlene Altman, Terrence N., & Steven J.—you all represent significant moments in my life. Please know that in your moment you were a vessel of hope, strength, and inspiration. I am a better person because of you. I am thankful to have been in your presence, even if for just that moment.

To my East Coast family and forever friends, Tanya, Byron, Guion, and Marissa—thank you for your acceptance and one hell of an experience. I can't wait to do it again.

Mommy—because you were the woman you were, I am the woman I am. Nothing will ever change that.

Foreword

I believe what initially draws individuals to the helping professions varies, but often has something to do with a passion to help others as a means of helping themselves or their family. It takes but seconds to realize that what drives individuals in the field regularly has roots in their own personal experiences. As if this field's work is not personal enough, the connection to our own roots can make our roles as clinicians a much more emotionally charged and overwhelming experience. The challenge is in knowing what level personal acknowledgement, awareness, and healing is necessary for each of us to do no harm while hopefully doing some good for others. While *Depressed People Make Me Sleepy* is an exquisite example of **M. J. Rex's** journey to figure this out, the themes lend themselves as a model to trigger self-exploration for countless others.

M. J. once stated, **"Out of the darkness came my joy."** Her truth represents what is possible when one makes the decision to venture out on the self-journey necessary to become an effective helping tool for others. These self-journeys, which are an implicit part of the training of psychologists, force us to ask on a deep level how it is we really know what we need until we have received it? In my experience, knowing this is how many of us will define true growth, which in itself is *Something Beautiful* and an amazing gift.

It is through the unexpected realization or corrective emotional gift that we have brief glimpses of clarity. What these glimpses reveal often seems to have been so obvious that one would think we should have known all along. As a trainer of future practitioners, I seek out future helpers with the perspective that, *a good practitioner is one who is always digging deep within their self to find what it means to be whole.* However, it isn't until we think we have become whole that we often realize we were functioning, on some level, attempting to navigate our experiences, as only *Half a Person.* This realization pushes us even harder.

It is important that people starting out in the helping profession be smart, cleaver, and curious. However, what I have seen over the countless years is that the person who is always willing to take a hard look at themselves in order to harness their strengths and humbly grow into their challenges is inevitably the most ethical, legal, and effective. I have had a good track record of selecting such people to be part of the training programs I run. With my own advice in mind, I was humbly wrong in my thinking but, correct with my intuition when it came time to work with **M. J.**

Not long ago when I initially met **M. J.** it was not under the best of circumstances. Although she was a new trainee at one of my sites, I was forced to meet with her to mediate and discuss the expectations of her time with our agency due to a matter that arose before she had even officially started. As I headed toward the pre-arranged meeting, I couldn't help but wonder, why it was I was having to spend my time talking to this psych intern about professionalism and conduct prior to even starting with our agency? I knew there was a story I was not yet privy to, but really, how could I be expected to help someone become successful in this field when they are so immersed in their own "*stuff*" that they can't even see how they're impacting others? It had crossed my mind, as a gatekeeper, that not only may she not be appropriate for this training site, but that she may not be appropriate for this profession either—dare I think "Self-Absorbed Interns Make Me Crabby". The only thing I was clear about was that I'd need to be very clear and direct about my expectations of her and the very real possibly that her time could be cut short before it had even begun.

I wish I could say the inspiring meeting that took place that day prior to the start of **M. J.'s** placement with me, my weekly one-on-one meetings month after month with her, or even something clever I had said somewhere in-between, was the turning point. I am sure now however this was not the case. **M. J.** had to reconcile for herself what was necessary to continue on in this field all the while reliving her past, dealing with the present, and planning for the future. Change is often categorized into elements or steps. ***Depressed People Make Me Sleepy*** is told as a step-wise approach to change. There are some predictable phases and steps that we go through but, it is more about timing and readiness then a function of schedule.

There were a lot of things I wanted to convey to **M. J.** to include, any clinician worth their weight realizes how narcissistic this profession is and that this profession requires one to commit to a life long journey of exploring humanity, while hopefully helping others and themselves along the way. *Stories* and *The Power of Words* shows us, in a very emotional way, that we really can't truly know anything about others in this world until we first know more about ourselves. Unless we do the work necessary to examine ourselves, we are doomed to fail at guiding our clients toward their dark spots and ultimately towards their change.

I have often heard that perfection occurs when it is unexpected. It is not something we can plan for. It is in the same manner that change too occurs. It is not only often unexpected, but is also unpredictable. We are reminded of this in *I'm ok*. Somewhere in the bravery and courage of re-experiencing the journey portrayed in *Depressed People Make Me Sleepy*, a corrective emotional and professional experience happened for **M. J.** Like me, I am sure you will be faced with re-experiencing and reliving times of self-reflection, sadness, elation and boredom in your own experiences while following this practitioner's journey in trying to figure it all out.

Steven H. Jellá MA, MFT, PsyD

I know her. I know her so well her name is tattooed on my arm. I vowed I'd never be like her again. That I'd never trade my heart for anything less than its true value. Although I never thought she'd stand tall again I realize now that it is often during our darkest times that we blossom. And that even when there doesn't appear to be an end to the bad times perseverance provides opportunity for growth and understanding. For that reason the person she was, however troubled she may have been, has become my mentor; my friend. She is the steady oak I've searched most of my life for. I feel her pain and cry her tears, but she has also proven her strength ten folds. She has made me better. For everything she has endured she deserves peace. I thank her for carrying that burden. For sacrificing so that I could lift my head again without any shame. She is the old me. She remains an important part of me; of who I am. Through her I was given strength, empowerment and ultimately my joy. She is and will forever be My Joy. These are the courses of her life.

M. J.

Depressed People Make Me Sleepy:

My Curriculum Vitae

Stories

I hate therapy. It's so hard to focus sometimes. I find myself sitting across from a stranger, who, despite my clearly uninterested blank stare and my "I couldn't care less about what you are saying to me right now" posture, is spilling his life story into my lap. I haven't always felt this way, but lately, since the death of my grandfather, I've been extra unfazed and uninterested in everything going on around me at home, at school, and at work. It has already been a few weeks, but I feel like he just died yesterday. He was the closest thing I had in recent years to my father's side of the family. He was also my last living grandparent. He's on my mind every day, and I miss him. But instead of grieving, I'm here listening to these stories. Some are real. Some fabricated. Nonetheless, everyone has a story to tell. Some people have way too many.

I'm in a one-on-one therapy session. I'm nodding and smiling, with an occasional *uh-huh*, but my mind is somewhere else. It's wandering around Neverland pondering all the things I'll never get done, at least not on time, like the paper I was supposed to turn in one week ago in school. I sat down at my computer the evening before it was due, staring at the blank computer screen, struggling to come up with something to write. I've forgotten papers before; twenty-five- and thirty-pagers. After having an *oh, shit* moment, I'd sit down and knock out what takes others weeks to do in a matter of hours. I always knew I was good at putting pen to paper. After winning several awards for my work, writing became more habitual and less about winning contests. I found myself writing all the time. It felt natural to me. I started out as a great bull-shitter just telling stories. Over time I got really good at putting real words down in a believable and engaging manner. People were drawn to my writing for some reason. That night, a week ago, for some reason it just wasn't coming to me. So, dreading having to tell my teacher that I, a third-year grad student who is expected to always be prepared and at this stage in her academic career should know better, decide to just not go to class at all.

I'm back from Neverland. He's still here, and he's still talking. He is also smiling. I'm confused by the inappropriately cheerful demeanor in one who is supposedly depressed. He told me during our walk earlier in the day that things were going well for him. He appears to be a helpful and extremely friendly guy. This throws me. I can't stop wondering why he's here. He is way too conversational and long-winded for me. This is supposed to be a thirty-minute check-in, and we're twenty minutes in. All I've asked so far is, "How are you doing today?" I want to ask him why he's here, but I'm scared. First, because I'm afraid he'll go on for another thirty minutes attempting to explain what would take most people only a few seconds. Second, I can't figure out how to phrase it so it doesn't come off as cold, harsh, and insensitive. So I zone out again. He reminds me of a patient I met during one of my first nights here, the night I thought I might have killed someone.

A client had come in, and I was the lucky person assigned to meet with him. He was depressed. Depressed clients were the worst. The truth is that depressed people make me sleepy, which made it hard to focus during individual therapy sessions. I'd had a string of depressed clients recently and was very quickly burning out. I was becoming uninterested and unprofessionally impassive about taking part in the dreadful discussion that seemed to play out every night over and over again. I don't know if it was my own personal experiences knowing people with depression, or if this was just a disorder that I for some unknown reason just didn't favor treating, but I was struggling, no doubt.

My mom suffered from depression. If I had to give my clinical opinion, I'd say one or both of my sisters suffer or have suffered from it as well. It bored me to watch people drag and mope around. It pained me to continuously have to be strong for everyone else, including these people here. The extra weight from carrying everyone else's baggage was becoming unbearable. I'd ask clients, "How are you feeling tonight?" As they began to tell me how unbearable their, in my opinion completely bearable, lives were, I'd feel myself being slowly dragged down some dark, gloomy hole, like the ones you pass on a cold New York sidewalk, the ones with the hot steam blowing out of them. I was taught to never walk on them because if you step on one, you risk falling through the grate that's supposed to separate you from whatever the heck is down there. My mom always said to my brothers, sisters, and I that if we stepped on one, we would fall through, hit our head, bleed out, and die before help could get to us. She also told me that if I sat on something cold in the winter I would get hemorrhoids. This, I would find out, is not true. But whatever. I believed everything she told me, including how unsafe it was to pick a fight with these covered pits. Yet even with all my certainty that what she told me was true, I find myself tonight practically holding this man's hand and jumping right in alongside him. Although it's my job to guide him, I want to tell him what to do. I want to tell him to just get to the point already and skip all the parts where he blows smoke up my ass. I'm so not in the mood for his exaggerations, his fabrications, or any other cries and attempts to get attention he may use.

I keep dozing off. I can't help but think about my own sad life. All the hot air in this room is making me sleepy. I'm trying to find my happy place, but I'm a student. There's no such thing as a happy place, at least not for me. I can't stop thinking about how long I've been in school. It has been my entire life; ever since I could talk and walk. This never-ending crusade to be the best has sucked the life out of me. School was supposed to make my life better, but over the past eleven or twelve years, it has done nothing but isolate, tire, and stress me. I've come close to tears several times in therapy sessions like this one thinking about the life full of fun, friends, and all the other exciting things I'd given up in exchange for a good education—all in the hopes of a better life. It really is depressing thinking about all the mischief I've missed out on. I'm alone in life. That's how I feel. I'm tired, I'm sad, and all this man can do right now in this moment is complain. He has nothing positive to say at all. I'm so annoyed. I have my own problems, and I'm not happy about a lot of things in my life. But I get up every day, put one foot in front of the other, and I get shit done. I have obligations: bills, school, colleagues, family and friends who depend on me. Life goes on. No one cares about your problems. I learned a long time ago that life slows down for no one.

I feel trapped in this cubby they dare to call an office. As if that's not enough, I'm stuck with someone who can't find one single thing to live for. I go down the list of questions that I have to ask but hate hearing the responses to. In my head I'm trying to figure out how to word things so that I don't come across as a counselor just following daily formalities, even though that's exactly what I'm doing. "Are you feeling better this evening... how would you rate your depression...and have you had any suicidal thoughts today?"

"Yes," he says in response to my last question. Now he's looking at me as if to say *your turn—now play along and ask me the next set of questions.* I sit there for a few seconds. It's quiet as we stare each other down. Silence has always been hard for me. I always interrupt an awkward silence by humming or asking a stupid question. Tonight I've decided to challenge myself to sit in this silence a little longer than usual without panicking or dazing off mentally. I can't do it, though, so I jump right in with another question.

"Do you have a plan?"

"Yes," he responds. Here we go again. He answers but then waits for me to ask what his plan is. Why can't he just tell me? Is this his way of trying to hold onto my attention for as long as he can? Maybe he is depressed. Maybe having my attention is the only thing in his pathetic world that is important to him right now. I can't help but wonder who I am and what I represent for him. In this very moment, how much does he really care about what I say and don't say to him? What does he think I can offer him that he can't provide for himself? I wish he would just come right out and tell me what I need to know so that we can get this moving along a little faster.

"What's your plan?" I ask.

"The same plan I've had for three years," he says, right on cue as if he knows exactly what he wants to say before I even ask the question. He's choosing his words carefully and dangling them in front of me a little at a time. I want them so that we can move on, but I also don't want to beg for them. This song and dance requires a lot of patience. Sadly, there isn't a patient bone in my body. I'm learning the tricks of the trade, all the ways to get what I want from clients. I'm also learning, however, that despite my efforts they give their responses in their own time. I'm still trying to accept that my time means nothing here, at least not to the depressed, attention-seeking clients trying to drain every ounce of ability I have to just smile and breathe. I often wonder if this is the right career path for me. After three years of graduate school, it seems a bit late to have a change of heart. But at least if I did change my mind, it would be a decision. Right now I seem to just be gliding along through life. I'm supposed to care about these people, but I can't get past my own baggage. How can I be of any use to others if I'm no use to myself? I'm starting to think everyone else's depression is rubbing off on me. Or maybe it's the other way around.

I ask him if he can be more specific about his plan. He says, "I'm going to drown myself in the ocean."

Really?! I've always had a problem with filtering what I say, especially when I'm annoyed. Right now, I'm annoyed. Sometimes my mind moves so fast that I find it impossible to keep up with it. I will eventually learn to take a moment before responding so that I can avoid what I'm about to do. I said eventually, which means not yet. So of course, in true fashion, I jump right in and say, "I don't think your plan is working." I tell him that after three years of having the same plan, he is still somehow sitting here with me talking about it. He stares at me blankly, and I stare right back, pretending that I didn't just hear myself say the most ridiculous thing a therapist could ever say to someone who is endorsing SI; suicidal ideation, especially someone with SI, intent, and a plan. I try to convince myself that I am being paradoxical and confrontational and that it's okay because these are completely acceptable therapeutic approaches.

I decide to go another route. "Do you know how long it takes to drown yourself?" I break the silence because once again it is way too damn quiet in here, and my body and mind can't handle it. I begin to rock my chair by pushing my feet against the floor. This causes my chair to not only sway up and down but to creak. I don't like the squeaking sound, so now I find myself adjusting, continuously shifting in my seat uncomfortably in an attempt to make the noise go away. All the while I stare down this annoying man and tap my pen on the notepad I'm holding the way made for TV Shrinks stereotypically do in old movies and TV sitcoms. The only thing I'm missing is ridiculously large glasses with thicker than necessary black frames that appear to swallow my face.

He finally speaks. "About three minutes, I guess," he says hesitantly.

I barely allow him time to complete his sentence before I jump on him. "Man that is a long time to be out there not being able to breathe and fighting the urge to just stand up and walk out of the water. What if you survive? What if you end up on life support, or what if you actually do drown, but a lifeguard brings you back to life? That's an awful experience to have to remember or even relive." I'm speaking in a conversational, matter-of-fact tone as if we are two old friends having a casual conversation or friendly debate about something trivial. He looks confused. I don't know if it's because of my reaction to him or because he's never actually considered any of the things I'm telling him, but there is silence again.

"What are you thinking right now?" I say, still fighting the silence monsters in this room.

"I don't know," he says. He admits that he has never really thought about any of this in much detail.

"Three minutes is a long time," I say. "It may not feel like it when you're having fun, but when you're in trouble, it's a very long time. I know this from experience. Three minutes can be quite terrifying under the wrong circumstances." He stares at me. I can't stand this song and dance any longer. I tell him that his time is up. Group therapy is getting ready to start in about five minutes. "Why don't you take a breather before you head to group, and we'll finish talking later."

He hesitates as he stares blankly at me. He then slowly gets up and leaves the room. I feel like he knows that I have no intention of meeting with him again tonight. I've had my fill of gloom for the evening. I don't want to meet with him or anyone else tonight.

When he walks out, I turn my chair toward the computer and sit there staring at the screen. I'm struggling to come up with something to write in his progress note. The longer I sit, the harder it becomes to not think about the consequences of my actions or lack thereof. A coworker walks into the office. I tell him that I think I've just killed a client.

"How?" he asks, looking puzzled. I can tell he's struggling to determine whether I'm joking or if I really think I've just killed someone. After all, if any of us did kill someone, it would be me. I tell him I think my client may have just realized, with my help, that his suicide plan isn't good enough. I think he might try to figure out another, possibly more efficient, way.

My coworker stands there staring at me for a minute before he walks to a free computer and starts typing his own note. He talks to me over his shoulder. "If he's going to do it, he'll do it with or without your help or permission," he says. "I wouldn't worry about it. You may have actually scared him out of it. If you feel that unsure about it, though, you can always just check in with him again after group."

This particular coworker is the cool white guy. I noticed him my first week working here because he always has on nice, name-brand sneakers even though he's an older gentleman. This is one of the benefits of having a son who works at a popular sneaker factory. He was also super willing to help me anytime I had a question, sometimes even when I didn't. No matter how much work he had, he was always available to me for consultation. I appreciated this more than he will ever know.

Tonight, however, I'm not really interested in his opinion, but I do appreciate it. I'm just looking for an out. If he didn't freak out about it, then why should I? Talking to him makes me feel better even though I didn't know I felt bad. I should have given that client my full, undivided attention, and I should have used acceptable therapeutic practices and made some effort to actually do some work with him, to process with him. I let the craziness of my own life outside of this the crisis house interfere with what could have been a life-changing intervention. Instead I offered him nothing. Telling my coworker, especially this specific coworker, makes me feel a little better, though. If I had done something wrong or something worth losing sleep over, he would definitely have told me. But I still don't feel that great about myself. I feel like I've just taken a burden that I created and placed it onto my coworker's shoulders. He deserves better. I find myself hoping that the client lives to tell his friends about my horrible counseling skills. I don't know if I can handle another death right now.

So here I am again with yet another depressed person. But he's a happy depressed person. That makes no sense whatsoever. He doesn't realize it, but he's totally talking at me. He has no idea that I've just completely dozed off and haven't actually heard a word he has said to me over the past forty minutes or so. How can people talk about themselves for this long? I'm suddenly staring him down cautiously. Something doesn't seem right, and I am so confused. I see his lips move. I watch him smile and cross his legs.

"My wife is the most loyal person I've ever known," he says. I find myself going from listening to nothing to listening to every other word to hearing everything. I'm focused on his appearance and the inconsistencies in his affect. As I listen more and more, I hear the saddest story ever. He's so self-aware, though—unusually so. He is painfully insightful. He knows that his life is sad, but he doesn't have the ability in his current state to fix it. His story intrigues me, and I'm leaning forward in his direction. I think I'm sad for him. How did I go from not being interested to feeling? I don't even know how I feel. I can't tell if it's sympathy or empathy.

What I do know is that I feel some kind of way for him. I feel for him in a way I've never felt for any other stranger who has sat across from me before. I want to hold his hand and tell him that he's doing a good job and that the fact that he is so self-aware and assertive puts him light years ahead of all the other zombies wondering the halls downstairs. Things will get better for him, and he's on his way to a much better life. But I can't.

It's not about me. Telling him that I care is my attempt to make myself feel better. I respect him enough to not want to patronize him. I can't promise him that he won't relapse, that his wife won't leave him, that things will get better. I can't promise him a single thing. But for the first time in a very long time, I am aware of how I feel. I don't like it. I'd prefer to be numb. Instead I feel helpless. I feel useless. I feel like he deserves better, a more seasoned therapist so that he can really get the help he needs. He's done everything that I've asked of him. He has completed his treatment plan goals and action steps in record time and kept himself busy creating new things to do to stay out of trouble and distract himself from his feelings of hopelessness. He's trying so hard. And on top of all of this, he's nice. He's nice and respectful to everyone, including me.

In all his days here at this crisis house, he has been helpful, going above and beyond to make this miserable place a home for everyone here. *He deserves better.* I don't know what it is about him, but when he gets up to leave the room, I find myself contemplating hugging him. He stops and glances over at me just long enough to thank me for my time and help.

My help? It was like doing something really mean to someone and then having them turn around and say *I forgive you.* That hurt. It didn't feel good at all. I was sick to my stomach. It was the first time that I had contemplated doing my job better. I had no desire to do therapy. My preference was assessments, which is why I went into forensics. Therapy was a necessary evil in my mind. I never cared about whether I was good at it or not. I might be able to get away with turning in assignments at school late and skipping class on occasion, but at the end of the day, did I really want people to look at me as that girl? The one who doesn't take her job seriously, who doesn't care what others think of her? The one who doesn't appreciate or respect the difficult and selfless task of putting others first, helping them to become their best. The girl who does crappy therapy and doesn't protect the lives entrusted to her? That's what therapy is about, selflessness. Was I capable of accepting this challenge? I want to take this more seriously. He made me want to be better. When he left I was stuck thinking just that—how can I be better? If I'm going to do this, I might as well do it as well as I can. I should really try to give it my all.

One Gift

My favorite Christmas was the year that my brothers, sister, and I all received one gift each. We sat up all night gathered in one room, laughing, joking, and carrying on about everything and nothing. I don't know what the joke was about, but I remember us all laughing ridiculously hard. We were all really close—my older sister, two brothers and I. My younger sister isn't born yet. We won't always be this close. As we grow older there will be tests that challenge and ultimately weaken our bonds to each other. They will eventually tear us apart. I am about thirteen or fourteen now.

I was a mini superstar. At least that was what I thought. I not only sang on the church choir but was known around my neighborhood and in school for my performances at local talent shows. I also performed at school for career day. My brothers and sister sang as well, but it was me and my older brother who had planned our entire life around the assumption we'd get a record deal and become huge stars. I also trained in dance along with my sister and wrote everything from poems to songs and speeches and competed competitively individually and with my school debate team. My mom was front and center at every essay and speech competition, science fair, dance recital, and talent show that I ever participated in. I enjoyed her consistency. She was the best mother ever. She even used to design the costumes for our dance performances, stitch by stitch, watch us practice, and then sit in the front row and transform into the world's best untrained, embarrassingly awesome, you-got-to-love-her cheerleader you've ever seen. She was proud of me, but I was equally as proud of her. So when I placed in a local writing competition at my school and advanced to the next level, which was state-wide, and was asked to write a speech about a hero, while everyone else wrote about the likes of Martin Luther King, Jr., and Rosa Parks, I wrote about her. And wouldn't you know it, I took third place.

The shock of my third place win out of hundreds of entries wasn't because they selected my presentation above so many others; it was because I had walked out of the competition just two hours earlier, feeling unprepared and nervous. It was Mrs. Altman, my favorite high school teacher, who came and got me from the hallway and worked her magic. She had a way of making me feel much smarter than I actually was. She sold me on things that I knew were untrue and outrageously exaggerated, but I always went along with it. Sometimes I felt like I had been duped afterward, but this was usually while bathing in the spoils of my success. She wasn't the reason I began to write, but she was the reason I got so darn good at it. Much more than a teacher, she was a pivotal figure in my young life. And over the next few years, she would become the glue that slowly pieced my broken soul back together. She would eventually breathe life back into me in a way that no one else at that time could. She reminded me of love even though I had never experienced real love from a stranger in my life. I had heard it once at church—love is patient, love is kind, does not brag, isn't arrogant, does not dishonor others, is not self-seeking. She was patient, kind, and warm, a protector who always had trust in our relationship and faith in me. My word was always good with her even when I didn't believe myself. For those reasons and so many more, I trusted her.

Mrs. Altman was a hopeful person who always brought out the best in me. She annoyed the hell out of me when we first met because she never got mad at anything. It was irritating to me how unmoved she was by the things that made everyone else's blood boil. Don't get me wrong—even though she was a petite, soft-spoken grandmother, she knew how to get your attention. She was undercover. Her appearance was cloaked in frailty, but underneath it all was a feistiness that only a cute old lady could get away with. If love was a real person, it was her. Her red, fiery hair only added to the superwoman illusion. The numbers tattooed on her arm only proved how resilient and unbreakable she truly was.

That morning was like every other Christmas morning. We bum-rushed the stairs, missing a few, trying not to fall before reaching the bottom. I had the biggest box. I was so excited that I could have sent myself into convulsions.

I ripped through the wrapping paper and stared at the machine, puzzled at first. My little brain was thinking so fast in that moment that it temporarily short-circuited, shutting down for a few seconds. I got a karaoke machine! It was mind-boggling. I was the happiest child in America. I already thought I was the next big "it," so now, with a karaoke machine, I was unstoppable. I could record myself acapella or over tracks with the dual recording system and cassette decks and practice with the microphone. The list of things that I could now do was endless.

For a long time, I didn't even know we were poor. We had about as much as everyone else. We were all poor, I guess. But when you grow up in a place where everyone borrows sugar or an egg or two every now and again, it's hard to notice that the rest of the world doesn't live this way. We spent several nights by candlelight. I remember being scared that I'd fall asleep and wake to our house burning down. Now, the thought of not having a candle burning in my home seems unimaginable. Who knew that lighting candles could be so soothing? Cold showers were a rare but occasional necessary form of self-torture. But it was counting out pennies so that we could go buy rolls of Scott toilet paper from the corner store that solidified my desire to be famous. I felt bad for my mom. I could feel her hurt, her disappointment about how life had treated her. Thus far she had been a rock, but I knew there had to be nights when she cried herself to sleep. I knew she wanted more for us.

I couldn't believe that my mother had gone out and bought me a karaoke machine. For a moment I sat and stared at it, contemplating how much money it must have cost and whether she used rolled pennies or actual cash. Money didn't make any sense to me when I was younger. I thought about money in objects, not dollar amounts. So this must have cost like a hundred rolls of toilet paper plus tax. I was torn. I loved my gift so much, but I wondered for a moment or two before taking it out of the box and plugging it in or even thanking my mom. Could she really afford this? How selfish was I to accept such a costly gift? I knew that this machine would only make me better and so bring me that much closer to getting my family out of this Section 8 house in this drug-infested neighborhood. I couldn't help but imagine how many extra shifts my mom would have to work, what bill didn't get paid, and what other miscellaneous things we would be giving up over the next few weeks and possibly even months. But she had done it again. Without saying a word, my mother had found a way to prove to me once again just how much she loved me and what my happiness meant to her.

Something Beautiful

God's crying. We are seated in the center of the living room on the floor. Old newspaper protects the hardwood surface from our crumbs. It's pitch black inside the house aside from the glow of candles and the occasional lightning strike. The living room door leading to the front porch is open. Soft music, the likes of Mahalia Jackson and Yolanda Adams, envelops us. We are afraid of the sound of thunder outside, but you wouldn't know it by the calmness in the room. There is a steady breeze flowing through the screen door. It stirs the smell of grilled cheese and tomato soup, Mom's cure-all for everything: illness, a fall, a bruised ego, and scary weather. No matter what it was, grilled cheese and tomato soup made it better.

The world was a scary place back then. In some ways it still is. Although there were demons outside of our home—racism, sexism, classism, to name a few—it would be the demons closest to us that would teach us, or at least me, the greatest life lessons. At that age we had no fears, thanks to our mother. She shielded us from it all. I didn't know if my mom was a good mom or not. There was no measuring stick for this type of thing. What I did know was that we had what we needed and were, for the most part, happy. Even when the lights were out or the water was shut off, we were happy. She always found a way to protect us from the chaos we were too young to understand. At least she tried to. This was the mom I loved and adored.

If I added the time we spent sitting and waiting, it would be days. But he doesn't come. It's his turn, his weekend, and his time to be with us, and as usual we are excited. Even though he didn't show the last time, there was always a chance that this week would be different. I always thought that he shared in our excitement. How could he not? I was young, but I couldn't imagine not seeing my own flesh and blood for days at a time. He was my flesh and blood, and it was hard to imaginegoing another week without seeing him again. I counted the days between visits. Not because I didn't have fun at my mom's house, but because visits with him were rare. It was like waiting for Christmas every year, only the time in-between was shorter. You know it's coming, and you'll probably get exactly what you asked for or some almost-can't-tell-it's-a-knock-off version, but you still can't help but be excited. For us Christmas came and went on the first and third weekends of every month. Most times, we got nothing. But we still sat on the porch, week after week, bags packed, high hopes in tow, sometimes for hours, and we waited.

I adored my father at that age. I'm not sure why. Fathers were rare. Most of my friends didn't have one, but I did. I used to tell myself that this made me special, that because my father actually cared enough to come around at all, I had a better chance at being someone important one day. I had always heard how not having a father made it more likely that you would get into trouble, end up in jail, or just be a no-good, noncontributing, useless person filling space in the world. Because he was a part of my life, I was different from all the nobodies running around my community.

My father didn't come around a lot, but when he did, I felt a need to connect with him. I wanted him in my life so bad. His inconsistent visits gave me hope that one day he would care for us, his children, the way we cared for him, that one day he would look forward to seeing us and being around us as much as we always looked forward to being with him. It was the worst feeling ever. If he had just told me he didn't want me in his life, I think I could have somehow moved on and got over him, but he didn't, and so I clung to all I had—the hope that he would come next time. This paralyzed me. I was stuck loving and hating him at the same time. I was bitter and resentful all the time. He found time for his new family, but not us. I wanted to blame them for his lack of interest, but the truth is he paid about the same amount of attention to us before they came into his life as he did afterward. He didn't change. They didn't change him. He was the same absentee father he had always been. He just also happened to be remarried and taking care of someone else's children now. My aunt and grandmother tried to make up for the time we'd lost with him, but they could never replace him. As I grew closer to my grandparents and aunt, their relationship with me, their modeling of what it meant to want to be there, just moved me further away from him.

We sit on the sofa at my father's house, just the two of us. It's the house we all grew up in.

My father, his brothers, and his sister all lived here as children and adults. Now, this house, passed from my grandparents to my father, has become our house as well. We all grew up here too. It feels just as much our house as theirs. This is neutral territory. My mother and father don't get along, but here we don't talk about our other life with Mom. She lives in a different state, but it might as well be another country. Everything is different. Here, we don't worry about the lights going out, the water or heat being shut off. We eat out more than at home. With Mom we eat out, usually hoagies, when the food stamps arrive once a month. Here, we could eat out anytime we wanted without feeling guilty or like we were giving up something else. We had video games, bikes, space outside to run free. At home we just had the porch. On the occasions we were allowed off the porch, we had to be back, either on the porch or the front steps, when it got dark. The streetlights, when they were working, were our cue. The rules here are different. Our lifestyle here is different. The burden of being the children of a single parent doesn't exist here.

I ask my dad why he doesn't call us, and he immediately responds, "Why can't you call me?" I explain that we are his children and he explains that he is our father. He says he doesn't like calling because of my mom, but I ask, pushing even further, "How can you let her keep you from us? Don't you ever wonder how we are doing?"

He responds, "Don't you ever wonder how I'm doing?" I feel like I'm talking to one of my siblings. I'm asking him questions that, as an adult, I hope my children never ask me. It would bother me, and I'd have to assume most parents, that my child didn't feel like I wanted to be in his or her life. It would bother me that my child felt invisible to me. It would bother me if my child expected to be stood up by me week after week because this was all she knew.

He appears to be completely unfazed by this. He tells me that I have his number and I can always call him. This is true, but what's the point if he doesn't call back? I'm not sure if I should continue this conversation or whatever it is we're having. I'm ruining our time together, what little time we have—or is he?

I never had to wonder where I stood with my mom. Her children always came first. If she had to pawn her jewelry or skip a meal herself so that we could have seconds, she didn't hesitate. There was no discussion. Our happiness, our needs, our futures—these were the things she held dear.

There was no time off, no break from feeding us, clothing us, and tending to our every need. She became a secondary figure in her own life. Her dreams were no longer her own, but ours. But I sit next to my father, and I don't know where I stand. We have nothing in common. There is no distance that could keep my mom from me, but I am right next to my father, and we couldn't be further apart.

We're back at home. The annual costume parade at school is coming up. We can't afford to buy costumes. I don't even say anything because I don't want my mom to feel bad for not being able to get anything for us. But as usual she is two steps ahead of us. I don't remember what I end up going as, but no one will ever forget my younger brother's costume. He is wearing green pantyhose and a cardboard box. His arms are dangling from the holes that Mom cut into the sides of the box, which is wrapped in Christmas wrapping paper. He is a Christmas present. He's embarrassed, but all the parents and teachers at school love it. I'm not surprised when he is called out of line as the entire school circles the recess yard one class at a time. He's won the most creative costume this year. Creativity should be my mom's middle name. Better yet, her first name should be hyphenated to include the name Creativity.

As winter approached that year, we found ourselves cooped up at home all day. Glued to the television watching cartoons was how we passed our time. We had gone weeks without seeing our father, but my mom always had ways to distract us.

I'm startled half to death when I feel something hit me in the back of my head, even more shocked to find that it's cold and wet. My brothers and sisters leap to their feet and start running. What I thought was a leaking ceiling is actually a snowball thrown by my mom. She's hiding behind a wall, and every few seconds, she sticks her head out and throws another one. She's still wearing her nightgown, and she has rollers in her hair and slippers on her feet. In her hand is a large, black stew pot that she has filled with snow from the back porch. We follow her lead and fill bowls and pots for ourselves, and an all-out, wet and wild snowball fight ensues—inside our house. Of course we spend hours cleaning after this, but we don't mind. Despite all the freedoms we had at my dad's house, it was here, where there wasn't much of anything aside from necessities, that I always had the most fun. We learned to depend on one another and that family was all we needed to have a good time. We didn't need bikes, big TVs or video games. There was no white room that we weren't allowed to enter with shoes on. We had free range here to be children, and we had one another. Most importantly, we never had to guess about our mom's loyalty to us. If I didn't know anything else, I knew that we, my brothers, sister, and I, were individually and as a unit loved by my mom.

When I had to prepare a culturally inspired arts and crafts project for school, I was nervous. My mom always came up with something unique. But that didn't always mean it would be cool. She and my aunt had once taught us how to make dusters with a metal hanger and colored yarn. They taught us tons of arts and crafts, goofy songs, and bad but funny habits, like how to hold a spoon on your nose with no hands.

I was having a hard time trying to figure out how a hanger duster would be an acceptable item to bring to class, especially since we had to make something from scratch that represented a culture other than our own. It would be pretty hard to make the argument that a tool used for dusting or cleaning wasn't directly associated with slavery or housekeepers, who in my very small world were all black. As the due date drew closer and closer, my mom kept saying, "'We'll get it done." I was becoming more nervous about the thought that I would be going to class with a hanger duster or friendship bracelet, which was something else that we had learned how to make, or, even worse, a seat cushion woven out of old newspaper and sealed with a shellac of glue and water. These were all cool for arts and crafts at home, but for a class project?

When Mom calls me into the living room the night before the project is due, I have never been more confused in my life. What the hell?! She's sitting on the floor with a brown paper bag, some wooden tongue depressors, and a lighter. We use brown paper bags to roll our hair up sometimes when we can't find our rollers, and the tongue depressors are typically for stirring a perm. The lighter is used to burn the ends of braids or light candles when the lights are out. I tried to put them together, and I got nothing.

"Go get the box of crayons and a bottle of glue," she tells me. When I come back, she's cutting the bag into a shape. She suddenly stops and begins making little folds. She hands the partially folded bag over to me and tells me to continue folding it like so. I do as I'm told. This way when it doesn't turn out right, I can say it's not my fault because I did as I was told. When I'm finished folding the bag, following instructions, I remove all the broken crayons from the crayon box as my mom lays a towel on the floor. She takes the pieces of crayons and starts to burn them. She has placed the folded, now unfolded, bag on top of the towel. She's holding the lighter with one hand and a crayon in the other and letting the colored wax drip all over the bag as she swings her hands back and forth from one end to the other. She switches crayons as I hand them to her. She asks me if I know what it is yet, and I have no idea.

When all the broken crayons have been used, and the bag is completely covered with surprisingly pretty swirls of color, she gives me a handful of tongue depressors and tells me where to glue them. When our brown bag, now covered with melted crayons and accessorized with tongue depressors, dries sometime later that evening after I've eaten dinner, my mom calls me in so that we can finish my project before I go off to bed.

I am dumbfounded by the finished project. Not only is it pretty, but it's functional. She put some more work into it while I ate dinner, but for the most part, this is our project. We did it together. Like so many nights before and after, she has once again pulled off a miracle. She explains to me the history behind my project, a traditional Chinese fan. I will of course brag about how much work and research I put into this project as I walk around school the next day playing with my fan, which I broke before I even got to present it in class. My mom always made a way out of no way and had an endless supply of cool ideas. This was just one of many projects that she worked on with one of her five children. To me it was another one of my greatest childhood memories and life lessons. It will forever remain an example of how good *simple* can be. More important, this is time that I will never forget—time that I spent with my mom making something beautiful.

Half a Person

"One, two, three, four, five, six." I'm counting out loud the way they taught us to in class. Somehow I imagine that this is a dummy and not someone I know. I've taken CPR classes several times. I don't remember why exactly. Maybe it was something I learned in the girl scouts and during health class in school. Never in a million years did I think I'd actually have to use it on my own brother. We found him hanging in his room a few minutes ago with a belt around his neck. I was the only one who took the class. I think my mom took it years ago too, but she was so hysterical. She was shouting for someone to get a knife or some scissors as she hugged his body, holding his weight and releasing the tension of the belt with her fingers. My sister came back with the scissors, and my mom cut the loop.

My mom yelled, "Did someone call 911?"

"It's busy," I remember my sister saying. I'm still counting. I'm on my knees next to his body, and my mom is attempting to breathe into his mouth. I remember thinking *911 can't be busy. Why would 911 be busy? How many other people can there really be at this very same moment with a real emergency? This isn't happening.*

Twenty-one, twenty-two, twenty-three, twenty-four, twenty-five, twenty-six. He's vomiting. We roll him onto his side. I see my sister at the entrance of the bedroom holding the phone. It's on speaker, and she has finally gotten through to 911, but she's on hold. My younger brother is in the background, hovering. Vomiting is good, isn't it? I'm looking everywhere but at what I'm doing. I'm here, and I'm going through the motions, but my mind is elsewhere. I'm trying to figure out how someone can hang himself from a bunk bed. What happened here? Am I doing this right? Where was my other brother when this happened? How high am I supposed to count? Thirty-two, thirty-three, thirty-four.

It takes what seems like an eternity. The paramedics finally arrive. The room is too small, and we can't all fit along with all the equipment they've brought along, so they ask my mom to leave as someone switches places with her and quickly slips a mask over my brother's face. I continue to pump at his chest and count. I make eye contact with one of the paramedics. Under any normal circumstances, this would be considered rude. But he knows that I'm looking for answers. Most important, I'm looking for reassurance, some sign that everything is going to be okay. They are all emotionless. Their faces give nothing away as they go about their tasks.

I'm surprised at my calm and lack of emotion. Maybe I'm simply mirroring the faces of the first responders. All I can think about as I press into his chest is how cool it'll be when he gets to tell everyone how he survived an accidental hanging. All I've had up to this point was a broken thumb and surgery to remove my tonsils. How the hell was I going to top this? We would one day sit and laugh about this. I don't know what parts of this would or could be funny, but I'm sure we will somehow find a way to get some twisted humor out of what's happening here tonight. As I am asked to leave the room, I see one of the workers cut my brother's shirt off. Instantly I think, *We can't afford that.* I mean, I've always been able to get up in the morning and find something to wear to school, but we didn't have much of anything to spare. We're in Section 8 housing, receiving food stamps every month. We barely get by. Even as children we knew when my mom received her state benefits and when to ask for what we needed because things would start to run low and then miraculously be replenished.

When food was low, my mom would start cooking weird things in bulk that weren't necessarily nasty but not something we would run to the kitchen to eat if there were other options. It was usually something from my mom's stockpile of canned stuff. Spam, Vienna sausages, beans. Put it over rice, and voilà. She used this same philosophy that anything is good over rice or in a soup when cooking meals for the homeless, which was something she did every few weeks. I wasn't sure what we were going to eat some nights, but somehow we always managed to make it to downtown Philadelphia to the corner of JFK. This is where the homeless congregated and where we handed out several crates of soup and bread. I think they liked it there because there were vents in the sidewalk that spit out hot air. It seemed an ideal place to keep warm on a cold night. Seeing this solidified what my mom would always tell us—no matter how little we had or how hard things got, someone else always had even less, and God would provide for us and never place more on us than we could bear.

It's not until I see his motionless body loaded into the ambulance, covered with white sheets and strapped down, that I realize how serious this is, and I begin to wonder for the first time how accidental this hanging really was. As the police come in, swarm the house, and question my mom, my sisters, younger brother, and I are ushered across the street to a neighbor's house. She is eager to take us in. A little too eager, I remember thinking. Her son has a crush on me. I am irritated because the neighbor is asking us what happened. Not because she's concerned, but because she is being nosy. Her empathy doesn't seem genuine. She's telling her son to give me a hug, to hold and comfort me. He has chestnut-brown eyes. I don't know why that bothered me, but there was something dishonest about his eyes. At this age I am a skinny and awkward fifteen-year-old. As much a geek as you could be without the high-water pants and glasses, and yet he thought I was pretty. There was nothing about me that I considered even remotely pretty. So for him to say I was made him a liar and therefore untrustworthy. He made me uncomfortable. When he stared at me with his chestnut-brown eyes, all I saw was deception. I didn't want him to touch me. I'm sitting on the sofa, and he sits next to me. I notice that even as I move slightly to put space between us, he continues to move closer. I'm upset that he is using this moment to come on to me. I am upset that his mother has encouraged it. I am mad because I am beginning to accept the possibility that this hanging is no accident.

Everyone is at the hospital. The Red Cross has somehow helped get my grandmother and father here. My father is crying. We are all standing around the hospital bed staring and crying as these very lively machines pump, suck, beep, and click as they attempt to breathe life back into my brother. I'm staring at my father. I can remember so many important moments in our lives: dance recitals, plays, performances with the band and choir, straight A's. My brother used to get straight A's. He also used to carry a suitcase instead of a book bag. I still don't know why my mother thought this was a good idea. She set him up to get teased and then pretended to be confused about why anyone in their right mind would tease a little kid with glasses and a suitcase in elementary school. As if any child at that age could resist the temptation to tease him. Of all these priceless moments, this is the one that my father shows up for. My brother will never even know he was here. Why the Red Cross wasted its resources is beyond me. I am annoyed by it. He has no right to cry. He's not losing anything or anyone. He doesn't have the moments, the fights, the failures or successes. He will never know his own son the way the rest of us do. He has none of those memories. But he cries. I wonder why.

When the doctor talks to the adults about pulling the plug, I wander into my brother's room. He is alone. I tell him that if he is going to get up, he must do it now because they are going to unplug his breathing machine. He doesn't move. A tear falls from his left eye. A nurse comes in, and I tell her that he is crying. She tells me it's the medicine that they put in his eyes.

I walk back across the hall as the nurse sets up materials for my mother to wash my brother as she did the day before. The adults are now concluding that they will indeed pull the plug. I go back to my brother's side. I'm alone with him. I take his left hand and ask him to get up. I explain that if he dies, I will no longer be able to say that I am a twin. Both of us need to be here on earth because that's the way God intended it to be. Why else would God give us each a partner at birth? Everyone else came alone. We came together. God must have intended for us to be together. I joke with God. *This must be your way of showing yourself,* I say. *When they come to turn these machines off, you will keep my brother breathing, won't you?*

I was into church. I did a book report on the bible. Read it cover to cover. We went to church all the time. We even put money in the tithes basket when we didn't have it to give. Sometimes we would even put change in the basket when my mom didn't have cash to give us. It was embarrassing. I was sure that God knew of our financial status and thus would give us a no-tithes pass from time to time. It was supposed to be ten percent of what we earned anyway, and we barely earned anything. But like clockwork every Sunday my mom would give us each a handful of pennies or whatever change she could scrounge up. We were members of several churches because we moved two times, going from one home to another before making my grandparents old home, in a third location, our own. We also weren't able to get to our home church because it was now too far and we lacked reliable transportation. With each home there was a new church. But no matter where we lived, church was a huge part of our lives, and I enjoyed going.

A sense of relief came over me as I spoke to God. I wasn't concerned. There was no way he would let my brother die. He made us twins. He couldn't take that away. He gave him to me and me to him. My brother was as much a part of me as I was of him. God had no right to change his mind and break us apart. He couldn't take back what wasn't his to take. This was my twin. We came into this world together, so I always assumed we would die together. A car crash, a plane crash—somehow together. I walk back across the hall, and the adults are all laughing and reminiscing about my brother's life as if he is already dead. I sit next to my mom and ask quietly, "Are they going to unplug the machines?"

She answers, "Yes."

"But he's not dead yet." She doesn't respond verbally. Instead she puts her right arm around me and continues talking with the adults. She will ask me tomorrow after his plug is pulled how I feel.

My response will be, "Like half a person."

I am sitting in the hallway near the elevators where my mom has placed us before the adults all went into my brother's room a few minutes ago.

Everyone has made peace with my brother and is with him as he stops breathing. Our minister gets off the elevator and speed walks toward my brother's room. A nurse comes out and says, "It's too late; he's gone." He stops short of my brother's room, hesitating before going in. I hear crying as he opens the door and enters.

I sit motionless. I think, *She killed him.* She really did it. How could she pull the plug on him? How could she just give up on him? How could any mom allow a doctor to talk her into giving up on her own child? And why didn't God show himself? Where's the miracle? I'm confused. My brother and sisters and I say nothing to one another. We don't even make eye contact. We're in the hallway alone. Have they forgotten we are here? I don't move. I feel alone. The hall is blurry. I sit still. Time sits still beside me. All the warmth and everything it represents have left my body. I'm shivering. I'm so cold. But I don't move. I don't know what to feel. I don't know how I am supposed to feel. In that moment I might as well have died too. I am physically, mentally, and emotionally cold, frozen in time, and officially half a person.

The Power of Words

I hurt all over. If you asked me to point to the pain, I wouldn't be able to. There is a constant throb that pulses through me. I have headaches, my back hurts for no reason, I'm always tired, I can't sleep, and I struggle to breathe. I haven't had a really good deep breath in a while. I tried yoga and meditation, but yoga is stressful. Trying to hold some random, uncomfortable position not meant for women my size while focusing on clearing my mind—it's not relaxing at all. And meditation—as soon as I close my eyes, I am faced with life. I'm not ready to deal with that yet.

Maybe there isn't anything wrong with me at all. I feel like I'm broken, but I can't quite figure out where or how. In past years I've felt as if the best of me had gone, leaving only the cold half behind. Maybe it's hypochondrias or somatization. I've tried to wipe it away, pray it away, wish it away, and sleep it away, but it stays. For years it hangs over me like a shadow, casting darkness and doubt on everything I do. It clouds my every thought. I can't think straight anymore. I'm paranoid. I have racing thoughts. I fear everything and everyone. I trust no one. Everyone is a liar. No one deserves my undivided attention or affection. And to sit still means I'm dead. I've wondered at times what it would feel like to just be, just sit still with my thoughts and deal with them, confront myself head on and be still in one moment to face it all—to just be.

I thought I knew love. It was the way my mother tucked me in at night, paid the rent on time, and made sure there was food on the table. It was an action, not a feeling. Love was the way you took care of someone. It was never about how you felt for them. When you love someone, you work hard to show it because actions speak louder than words. When I got married at the age of twenty-two, that was what I did. I cooked the meals, or at least pretended to, washed the clothes, and made sure the house was always clean. I spent an incalculable amount of money building a life that my husband and I could be proud of and comfortable in. I showered him with love: clothes, vacations, filet mignon, and lobster (even though I'm allergic to seafood). I needed to be able to show him that I cared, and this was the only way that I knew how.

I married him because he asked me to. Up to that point, we'd had fun together and enjoyed each other's company, so why not? I believed the action of going through with the ceremony, even though everything in me said not to, would show him that I loved him, not the actual vows or the words "I do." The truth is, I didn't. I didn't believe in marriage, and I never saw myself going through with it. And although I would have loved him forever, I was also never in love with him. But here I was, and the only way to prove my allegiance to this person that I'd spent so much of my time with over the past year or two was to do it—just say "I do." And so I did, and I loved him the only way I knew how to.

Love, in the traditional sense, had never been modeled for me. When my father showed up, it was out of obligation. My mom took care of us because she had no other choice and it was her responsibility. I saw couples who fought like cats and dogs, but they stayed together because that was what you were supposed to do. The closest thing to real love that I saw was on television: Ricky and Lucy Ricardo, Mike and

Carol Brady—hell, even Roseanne and Dan Conner appeared to be in love. But because it was on television, I knew it couldn't be real. I never knew you were supposed to actually feel something, that you could lean toward someone even when they were miles away. That you could yearn to be near someone so much that it hurt or that people could love so much in life that they would literally die from heartbreak if their loved one moved on without them.

I've had so many clients sit across from me trying to convince me that heart break is the cause of their sadness and depression. What the hell does that even mean?! Why or how a divorce, breakup, or death could have such a significant impact on someone's ability and desire to live is incomprehensible to me. I've never been connected to anyone in a way that would allow me to relate to this kind of pain. There were many nights when I missed my dad or my brother, when I felt unsupported, abandoned, or alone. There was no time to cry. It never changed anything, and no one ever cared about my tears, so I learned to keep them to myself. Being down or crying in front of me is a waste of time. I can't relate to it. I'm the wrong person to be emotional in front of. I don't know what to say or how to respond. An awkward smile or giggle is all I have to offer those who cry in my presence. When it's a full-on ugly cry, I find myself irritated and sometimes even mad. I don't know why. I just don't get why people can't get over things the way I always have.

It was curiosity that drove me from communications and American literature to psychology. I already knew that I could write. I didn't need a piece of paper to tell me that I understood the evolution of words, their impact and value. I had been writing songs and poetry from the moment I knew how to write my own name. I needed something new. I wanted to learn how to formulate words in a way that helped me say what I felt and wished I could feel. What I know but don't understand. And what I need but don't want because I don't know how to accept it. A new way to express myself aside from poetry and song was what I sought. I wanted to continue to write but without melody. Melody reminded me of what I had lost. I was tired of remembering. I was looking for an outlet and a way to grieve, and the only thing I knew was music and lyrics. I gradually moved toward essays and speeches. I had been in so many essay competitions and joined the debate team. Words made me a winner.

I loved that I could use them to move people. More important, I loved that I knew how to use words to hurt people when necessary. There is a power in words that strengthens me. I knew how to make words cut like a knife, and I was empowered by this and proud of it.

I had a lot on my plate, and I was a lot more stressed out than usual. My brother had been dead for a little over twelve years and my family still hasn't recovered from this. His death slowly eroded the bonds that held and strengthened my family. We were all dealing with it individually, but not together. For the first time ever, instead of coming together like a family, we were divided. We weren't getting along the way we had in past years. Walking around smiling all day and pretending that life was all peaches and cream was beginning to wear on me.

My sister and I had been fighting back and forth, and I was tired of the tug-of-war, sick of the disrespect. I was tired of being talked down to and treated as if I were some insignificant figure off the streets who didn't matter to her. I had received the same treatment from my husband and other family members. I wasn't happy in my own house. I couldn't even call my family for support. I couldn't understand why people thought it was okay to talk to me however they chose. I couldn't understand why I allowed it. For years I sat quietly and let my own family and those closest to me do what I would never allow my friends to do to me.

It was my therapist who posed the question, "Would you allow your friends to treat you the way your family does?" "Are these the characteristics that you welcome into your circle?" Huh? She asked as if I had a choice. As if I could simply turn my family on and off or disown them just because they were asses to me. It was the same with my husband. I had said, "I do," after all. You can't just walk away from that. My word has always been my number one pride and joy, the thing that I was the most proud of and that most everyone could agree on when it came to the kind of person I was and still am: trustworthy, fiercely loyal, honest, and passionate. And when I gave my word, it meant just that. My friends all knew that my word was good. To suddenly say *I give up, I take it all back,* or *I don't want this anymore* was out of the question. Or at least it always had been.

You don't turn your back on your family. I wasn't raised that way. That's why I was so upset with my brother. I hadn't been able to understand how he could hang himself. It just didn't feel right. I was angry at him because, if this was no accident, then he was a selfish son of a bitch. It was the beginning of the end of the perfect life I thought we all had. His death had also destroyed any shot we had in the field of entertainment. We were supposed to make it together. It wasn't the same without him.

My mom changed drastically. My siblings and I had all changed. Everything had slowly begun to change for the worse, and nothing was as it was before his death. How could he not anticipate our pain or anticipate it and still be able to do this to us? Was he mad at one of us? Was there a sign that I had missed? Was he dealing with something that was so bad that he believed he couldn't come to us? If his death was an accident, then how could I not take some responsibility for it? How could I live with the burden of never knowing if he had called out for help and I hadn't heard? Whether I got to him fast enough, and if this would have made a difference? Whether he thought I was a good sister and friend to him? How could I not wonder if at some point reality kicked in, he knew he was dying, and he was scared? Or if I had done CPR correctly, and if not, if this had contributed in any way to his death? How was I supposed to ever get over this without knowing which one it was; an accident or deliberate?

It didn't take much for my older sister to set me off. She chose the wrong day to be a bitch to me. I had words on my side. I wrote her a letter. I wanted her to be able to refer to it for years to come each time she thought it would be okay to annoy me or disrespect me, to treat me as she had done for so many years. I told her, among other things, that I wished it was she who had died instead of my brother. I was mad at her, pissed off beyond reason. Even though I enjoyed spending time with her, I didn't like the person that she had become. She was a codependent, annoying, entitled, self-absorbed bully. She never supported me when we were younger and now when I need her most the reality of this hits me even more. She was never the sister I needed her to be to me. I worked so hard to get her to like me. My own sister—and I was working overtime just to be her friend. I'd had three graduations at this point. She never came to a single one or congratulated me. And even though I wasn't happy in my marriage, I hated that she disrespected my husband. I hated that I was missing my brother, who had been cheated out of so much by dying so young and here she was wasting her life away chasing after boys and being a bitch. I wish I could have seen her cry as she read the letter I wrote to her. Maybe seeing her in pain would have eased the pain I felt. To tell the truth, I don't know if it was really about her. But I was mad, so it didn't matter. I sent the letter.

Years would pass before we would speak again, and our relationship would never be the same, but I was fine with that. I had endured so many years of being teased and talked about, being the butt of the jokes, looked down on and isolated from family and friends because of things she would say and do. In my eyes I had won. Even if it meant never seeing her again; I had won.

Before my brother died there were five of us, but I always felt like the odd man out. My twin clicked with my older sister and was emulated by my younger brother who chased behind him. When my younger sister came along, she was everyone's new toy. Everyone had a purpose except for me, the middle child. I served no purpose at all. I'm also the only child to not be named after anyone in the family. I don't know if this was done on purpose, but I used to wonder why I didn't carry someone else's name like the rest of my brothers and sisters did. I was picked on by my siblings for being the goody-two-shoes, the favorite, the geek, the weird dresser, and the snitch, even though I really wasn't. They were always too stupid to get away with anything, but I was always to blame each time they got in trouble. I've always felt like a black sheep. Being a twin kept me connected. It made me part of the family. After my twin died, the divide only grew bigger. After all those years growing up as the forgotten child and then becoming the unsupported, invisible wife who gave and gave but always felt unappreciated and unnoticed, I was ready to speak up for myself.

I had slowly begun to cut people down, to clear my corner until there was no one left. No sister, no husband, and very few friends. I don't miss them. I sometimes miss the idea of what their roles in my life used to be, and I am aware of the empty space they used to fill. But if all they had to offer was never keeping their word, not being by my side when I needed them the most, using me, not involving me, and making me feel like shit all the time, then who needs them anyway?

For so many years I was stuck in this rut, letting people beat me down. I was wearing thin and feeling incomplete and lost. I took care of everyone else. I catered to everyone else's feelings and needs. I didn't know how to say no anymore even when I had nothing to give. I didn't want to take care of anyone anymore. If this was what it means to love and be in love or to feel, I didn't want anything to do with it.

Because I had stopped singing, I lost my voice. Now I was ready to get it back, and I had seen my own power—the power to use words in a way that no one else I knew could. I knew I would never make it as a medical doctor as I had once hoped, but with the right combination of words I figured I could move people to action, change their lives. I could help people find their purpose again, find their voice like I had done. For the first time since my brother died, I was using words again, the way I had in song. And I was changing lives. I couldn't fix myself, but the idea that I could fix everyone else around me kept me sane. Psychology allows me to use words in a way that I never have before. I am happy here. Psychology makes me feel normal again. It brings peace to my home.

Dirty Laundry

I see her bruises. They are deep red and purple marks that cover parts of her thighs and arms. When I ask her how she got them, she speaks as if we are talking about the weather. I don't know if she felt that she deserved this, or if it was just such a usual occurrence for her that the shock, secrecy, and shame of it, if there had ever been any, had long since gone. Maybe she has also forgotten that a man, especially your own husband, shouldn't hit you. Her "what's the big deal" attitude makes me feel as if she doesn't grasp this concept. Sometime later when I tell her that my husband too had hit me, she responds by asking me what I did.

"I hit him back the first time," I say.

"No, what did you do to make him hit you?" she casually asks. "He wouldn't have just hit you for no reason." She has somehow managed to normalize her own abuse, but that doesn't give her the right to downplay mine. Even though my experience was nothing like hers, as if I could know her experience, I knew that my husband's occasional blow-ups were nothing I wanted to accept as a permanent part of my life.

The thought that I would have to live the rest of my life fearing someone I lived with, never knowing when his temper would flare or the toll his lapses in self-control would cause was scary. Never knowing when his anger would interject itself into our lives was uncomfortable, to say the least. I was miserable and disappointed in both him and myself. We were so much better than this. We were supposed to be a successful power couple. We were supposed to support each other and lift each other up, not break each other down. My ego and self-esteem at home took a huge hit. And I was angry—all day, everyday. Even on my good days, I was down on myself. I had tried but failed to mimic my professional success at home. I worked hard to make my husband happy and prove to him where my loyalty was and how seriously I took my vows. It had crossed my mind a time or two that we were too young, that he might not be the one, but mistake or not—I was invested.

I haven't eaten all day. For the second day in a row, I have made a conscious decision to starve myself. I've just weighed myself for the third time. The first time was as soon as I got up this morning. The second happened immediately after my morning bathroom break. All I've had today is water, and I've had so much that I can feel and hear it swishing around in my stomach. It makes me feel fat, so I down two Ex-Lax. I'd make myself throw up, but I can't stand the sight of vomit. I don't think I'm obese, but I can stand to lose a few pounds, and I can definitely use some toning. I've tried dieting and exercise, but my schedule makes it hard to do both consistently. That's my life—helping others change their lives although I can't even fix my own. I guess that's the sacrifice we clinicians make.

I didn't begin to gain weight until after two surgeries put me out of commission around two-thousand and two. I just assumed I would flatten back out and shrink down to the size six figure I was accustomed to. School, work, and being everything to everybody but myself helped keep me an oversized version of a person who had long since disappeared. Today I'm working with a personal trainer. It's 5am, and I'd rather be asleep or lying in bed pretending to be. But it's the only time I have to myself now. The rest of my time belongs to strangers—individuals and groups of people who don't know me and couldn't care less about what keeps me up at night. I've done everything my trainer has told me to do. I haven't lost a single pound. I haven't gained either. Maybe it's the water. I guess I should at least be happy about not gaining. If I'm not losing, I definitely don't want to gain, but when is the last time you ever celebrated failing? I'm smart, funny, energetic, assertive, independent, and engaging—when I want to be. My younger sister and I have often joked that while she got the looks, I got the brains. I was proud of this fact. Right now, however, I'd trade it all to be a few pounds thinner.

I was content with my weight gain initially. I always thought I was way too tall to be as thin as I was at a boob- and butt-less size six and liked that I had filled out in areas my friends and family used to say were either flat or nonexistent. I was an invisible size six, and now I am a very visible fourteen. I liked it. It would have been nice to drop back down to a toned size ten or twelve, but anything smaller than that was too small for my liking.

After being called fat a few times a week by my husband, I had become insecure. I was willing to do anything to lose the weight. I was tearing myself down, at war with myself and fighting a losing battle. Everyday I'd find some new imperfection. At some point he didn't even have to put me down anymore. I did it to myself. A once self-confident, assertive woman proud of all my accomplishments and the obstacles I'd successfully overcome, and now I was struggling to find my own value. In his eyes I was worthless, so in my eyes that was what I became. I don't even know who I am anymore. When I'm working I'm too busy to be affected by how disappointed and displeased I am in myself. I love who I am at work on most days when I can keep my attitude in check, but at home it's just me and him. I hate going home.

I was away from home seventeen or more hours a day on average. Work, school, running a business, volunteering, and then back home to him. I somehow found the time to prepare his meals, clean his clothing, and keep the house in order. I wore lingerie I didn't feel comfortable in and made myself available even when I was unwell, hungry, or too tired. I made an effort to ask him how his day was, knowing I wouldn't understand a thing he told me about his job as an engineer. I even learned the names of his favorite soccer teams and watched matches with him instead of doing homework or getting much-needed sleep. I bought him tickets to a huge tournament that came to the area every year even though it fell on or around Valentine's Day and meant sacrificing the holiday to him and his friends and spending the holiday alone. I put his needs and wants, at least most of them, before my own.

However small he felt in what I would later recognize as my own shadow was not due to a lack of effort on my part. Maybe I didn't give him what he wanted, but if putting my education and career on hold to run a household was what he wanted, I couldn't give him that. I ran myself ragged trying to keep us together, but my big sister, whom I finally decided to turn to for help and advice, made me feel as if I were the problem. She said I was not a good wife and that because I sucked at providing for my husband somehow, it meant he had the right to objectify and discipline me. All she did was encourage me to stop doing whatever it was that made him hit me. I didn't sign up for this with her or him.

Although I was unsure exactly how I felt about my husband at this point, I hated her. I was raised to never discuss what goes on in my house in the streets. It was hard to ignore the voice in my head telling me to keep quiet. But when I finally broke down and asked for help after having never told a soul, I expected guidance, and all she did was push me down even further. Did she have any idea how hard it was for me to ask for help? How hard it was to go to work every day and put everyone else's needs before my own, to not have a single person looking out for me? I'd hid my bruises well up to this point, but enough was enough. I was tired of being scolded everywhere I went. How can someone put their hands on me and still make me feel as if I were the one who was insensitive, selfish, and inconsiderate? And how could she be too selfish to look outside of her own matters to be the big sister that I needed? If my own flesh and blood believed that I deserved this, that I had brought this on myself, that I was attempting to blow something that she believed to be a minor marital dispute into something much bigger than it was, my lips were sealed. I vowed never to speak of this matter ever again. He needed help, we needed help, but putting a spotlight on our relationship, our private lives behind closed doors, risking his career, his personal and professional relationships? How much sense did that make? I kept my mouth shut for years after this, and I willingly ignored the signs that I was in danger. I ignored the fact that my husband, the man who said he loved me, needed help and would probably never change.

I was living within a cycle of abuse that I couldn't escape. During the day I was everyone's yes person, as good an employee and employer as I could be under the circumstances. At lunch time, instead of eating with my colleagues, I always had a call to make, an errand to run, or something important that needed to get done before I continued on with my day. This was how I explained not eating when others were around. At the end of the day, I'd go home and binge. Not every night, but I'd do it at least once a week after having gone several days without much of anything. My husband's business trips were my time to eat all the things I would never eat in front of him. In fact, I rarely ate in front of him at all. If I was hungry, I ate in my car before I got home so that if we did eat together I could eat as little as necessary and still be full.

It didn't make much sense. I considered that this was why I wasn't losing weight. I went to the gym to meet my trainer and show him or her my fake food log. I was proud of the effort and detail that I had put into it. It only exemplified my ability to make everything appear exactly as I desired. I went through my workouts feeling faint but pretending to be okay. I worked out through blurry vision, painful headaches, and being so weak that it took all the strength I had to stand or lift my head. But I did well at this. I learned years ago that I have a pretty high pain threshold. Years of military training had built me up strong and sturdy. I learned to keep a straight face regardless of how I felt on the inside. I was a good student in the gym, pushing myself through pain and doing more reps than my trainers expected. So when I did have an off day, it helped sell the idea that I really just wasn't feeling well versus seconds away from passing out from starvation and dehydration. At my lowest point, I lost about fourteen pounds in a matter of a few days. I remember standing before the mirror naked and thinking that the loss had made the abuse all worth it. That somehow it had motivated me to push far past what I thought was my breaking point. I had found strength in my darkest hour. I was proud of myself for this. It made me feel strong and gave me a false sense of control.

It wasn't until my eyesight began to fade, the headaches wouldn't stop, and bingeing didn't seem as easy as it used to be that I even suspected something might be wrong. I was also often lightheaded and even though I was losing weight, I felt heavy and found it hard to exert myself for long periods of time without getting dizzy and needing a break. I felt so bad about myself that being around normal people was becoming impossible. I was ignoring my own needs in order to manage the needs of others. And I was in denial. I wasn't a battered woman. I was someone whose husband hit her a few times. There was a difference. I had mood swings that were out of character, even for me. I was fighting for every moment, crawling through my days, and it was getting old fast. I was tired of feeling weak but pretending to be strong, tired of waiting for changes that didn't seem likely.

My work left me hopeful. Every now and again, there would be that one patient or client who just made me feel like anything was possible. Watching them overcome horrible circumstances in their own lives and seeing the benefits of therapy gave me so much hope. If they can believe, then why shouldn't I? This was when being a therapist became my curse. I used to believe therapy could fix anything.

I didn't know how or when to let go. I would have given anything to be happy and not have to lie my way through each day. I would have settled for accepting myself for who I was so that I didn't have to work as hard as I did to change myself.

I was content with my decision to stay with my husband, but my perspective on love and relationships was forever changed. I tried to be good when I was in my husband's presence, but having to walk on eggshells was making me feel like a coward, which made me angry and bitter. I found myself watching weekend marathons of *Snapped* and *I Almost Got Away with It*. I was obsessing over the stories of the women who had murdered or attempted to murder their own spouses and the many ways criminals had avoided capture after committing their offenses. Seemingly normal people doing unheard-of things to the people they cared for—all in the name of love. I didn't want to be that person, but I understood it. I had grown cold inside and distant on the outside.

People saw us as the happy and funny couple who had everything to look forward to. In reality, we slept in separate rooms often, barely spoke, and avoided each other like the plague. My friends didn't like him. His friends were always reminding him how different I was from their traditional wives. We came from two different worlds: me, born and raised in a country where women were allowed to dream big, wear pants, and take care of themselves, and him from a place I'd never been to that was apparently full of submissive women who didn't mind staying home or allowing their men to be the dominant force in their homes. This was according to him, of course. I prayed some nights that he wouldn't come home from work, that I would get a phone call saying he had been in a horrific car accident and didn't make it and that I needed to give permission to pull his life support, which I'd do without hesitation. I imagined what it would be like to have to conjure up some fake tears and pretend to be devastated. How I would call his mother to tell her that her only son was dead, without laughing. I was tormented by my own indecisiveness to stay or go.

My decision to stay was eating me alive, but I did not want to be the one to throw in the towel. I never wanted to look back and realize I hadn't given it my all. I wanted out, but I didn't have the sense to leave until things were bad—really bad. Unfortunately, it was during these times that I was too beat down emotionally to make any decisions at all. By the time I got my strength and courage back to leave, we were on an upswing again. He made it impossible for me to stay, but his apologies, the flowers, and the minimal but seemingly sincere efforts to mend things also made it impossible for me to leave.

It was—still is—hard to comprehend how someone, the closest person to me, could hurt me so much. Although I was a certified domestic violence treatment provider, *how about the irony in that*, I found it hard to truly grasp the battle I was fighting. I was surviving, but it was hard. The physical pain was nothing, but the psychological effects were an entirely different beast. I was battered in so many ways, but he didn't get it. He tore me down but expected only the best of me. He couldn't understand what he was doing to me, and I couldn't tell him in a way that would make him understand.

He hated to see me cry. I would cry, and he'd be remorseful. I should have known the day he got mad instead of remorseful that we were done. But like every other red flag in our relationship, I ignored this. And I couldn't ask for help. My family didn't care; they had their own issues. The two times I'd called the police, I was told to just let him walk it off. One officer even said to me,

"You don't want to ruin his life over a mistake, do you?" I was mad at my family for not caring, mad at my friends for not noticing, and mad at myself for being so damn naïve and pathetic. I was stuck in every sense of the word.

The end was near. I didn't know what the final curtain call would be like, but I knew it was coming. There was no way we could go on this way. I wanted him to mess up really bad. I didn't want to die, but I was also tired of living this way. There were times when I thought he'd choke me for just a little too long, he'd hit my head just a little too hard, or he would get so mad that he would just stab me to death in a rage, and that would be it. All of our dirty laundry would be exposed because he'd have to explain to his family, my family, and the rest of the world what happened. There were no words that he could ever say and nothing he could ever do to undo what he'd done to me, to my spirit. But making him accountable somehow seemed a fair trade. The thought used to frighten me, that he could kill me, but when it no longer did, I knew something had to give. He didn't have to kill me at this point because I was doing more damage to myself than he ever could. We had lived this way for far too long. I had protected him for far too long. He didn't even appreciate that.

A few years later, when my younger sister confided in me that she too was in an abusive relationship, I was crushed and scared for her. I was sick to my stomach. Three sisters who couldn't be any more different, and we were all living the same life. We were each in our own corner of the world fighting the same demon— the man we loved.

Depressed

I wasn't sure if the patient met the requirement for major depressive disorder, or MDD for short. I kept staring at him. He said nothing, just sat there slumped in the chair staring at the floor. Every few minutes he adjusted himself in the seat and stared up at me. As soon as it was clear that my eyes were still fixed on him, he quickly looked away. Any other day I would just make the diagnosis and go about my business.

I didn't like being forced to quickly label people after spending only a few hours with them, but it was part of the job and something that I had become used to doing. Even if I wasn't sure what diagnosis to give, every client had to have one in order to be admitted. Most times it was obvious, but even when it wasn't, they still got one.

I still had three other clients to see, but for some reason, today I couldn't just label this man. I couldn't sum his life up in one or two words. I found this more insulting than my momentary lack of interest and sincerity, crueler than my urge to just slap a tag on him and move on to something more enjoyable. I couldn't get past the very specific complaints, the perfectly worded descriptions of his symptoms, and the seriousness in his threats.

Malingering. I couldn't get it out of my head. He appeared so perfectly sick that I found it hard to believe and understand how anyone could present this way. How could anyone let himself get this sick? This can't be real. He has to be faking. I couldn't relate to him. I was searching really hard for a sentence, a word—anything that could bridge the gap between him, the helpless patient, and me, the troubled therapist and only one who could help him.

I was back in group therapy class hearing my teacher's words: *You should always be able to find at least one thing that is relatable to everyone you come into contact with.* And yet here we sat, locked in what seemed to be two completely separate worlds with not a single thing in common.

His eyes played a game of hide-and-seek with mine. It reminded me of a drill I participated in when I was in the military. I hear myself silently chanting, "I'm up; they see me; I'm down." I had never worked so hard to connect with someone, but the harder I tried, the harder I sank into my head and my own troubles, making it harder with each second that passed.

"Are you hungry?" I was looking for an out, and I could smell the mélange of flavors soon to be plated together for dinner coming through the vents. The tiny office was right above the kitchen. I could hear voices coming through the floor, smell the food cooking, and hear the sounds of pots and pans beneath me. I figured I'd send this guy to dinner while I gathered myself and visited the *Diagnostic and Statistical Manual of Mental Disorders*, also known as the *DSM*, the mental health clinician's bible. Right about now I'd take any excuse to get rid of this man. I'm almost tempted to pull the fire alarm, but that would be a bit extreme, so I send him to dinner instead. And of course he goes, because even people who say they want to die get hungry, and who am I to let him starve to death?

That's not the way he wants to go, after all. I never could understand how suicidal patients could have the wherewithal to be picky about how things ended. I'd find the quickest, most efficient way and get it done. But that's just it. I couldn't relate at all. I fear death. Not dying, but the when and how. I've thought about how I would die before: my hit-and-run car crash in the early 2000s, watching 9/11 unfold on television in my squadron's ready room, my last relationship. Yeah, I thought about it, but never from the stance of actually taking my own life.

On a typical day, I'd sit with a client for a few minutes and let him do most if not all the talking. The more they spoke, the easier it became to make a clear diagnosis. Even those who declared that nothing was wrong with them painted pictures with their behavior and words or lack thereof. Sometimes I'd be thrown by deceptive comments, someone who was flat-out lying or deliberately omitting key facts such as past drug use or hospitalizations, or by a poor historian who left out other key details. But the diagnosis, that was always something that the client gave to me, not something that I, with all my education, experience, and intelligence managed to magically produce all by myself.

This guy, however, he barely said a word. Who doesn't like to talk about himself? Everyone who came through these doors loved to talk, especially about themselves, but lately people seemed to just sit and stare.

Today it was a new face, same story. I don't know if it was the chill outside or the impending holidays, but more and more people like this guy and the one I just got rid of had been showing up at our doors. I was turned off by their sadness, their silence, and the idea that these men, who clearly had much to be thankful for, truly believed they had nothing to live for. "You're a selfish son of a bitch," is all that comes to mind as I sit and stare at this man. We're past the awkward introductions, and he's finally speaking. I silently scold myself to be careful what you ask for. Now that he's found his voice, all he wants to talk about is his daughter, whom he apparently loves so much it hurts. Yet in the same breath he uses to proclaim his love for his only child, he tries to convince me that he has nothing to live for. I find myself wishing he would just shut up.

When I ask him if he has thoughts of hurting himself, I find myself internally answering for him, *Of course you do,* as I wait for him to say the words. "How?" I ask him. It was vague, but suicidal ideation nonetheless. I stop taking notes. His words, my words, they have become a routine that I am all too familiar with. I give the cue, he says the right thing, and I respond by asking him to contract for safety, which they always typically do.

I flipped through the *DSM* looking for the page that would make things clear. All I had to do was read the criteria and check off each qualifier that applied. The funny thing was that I already knew what my report would say. I was going to march right over to the computer and enter the same diagnosis that I was pretending not to know the criteria for. I knew it. I knew it like the back of my hand. There had been so many of them in the past few weeks, so many just like him. I had this act memorized.

When I first started working here at the crisis house I was assigned to for my second year of practicum, I was proud of myself for being able to slap the correct label on people. I consulted the *DSM* on occasion, but almost never. I saw so many people come through these doors. At the end of the day, it was always the same story, and the ending almost never changed. It was always some variation of two or three different choices. Sometimes I felt like this song and dance we did was so unnecessary. We'd take people in, bandage them up, and then send them back to the streets, where they'd open their sores back up and wander back to us for rebandaging. We were a short-term, revolving door of hopelessness, helplessness, desperation, and loss. Everyone had a loss, a precipitating factor, a trigger. They had somehow all discovered the trip wire that had been set for them many years before. They were all set up to fail, and there was nothing they could have done to change it. The only thing finding that trip wire did was lead them here. And it was always someone else's fault. According to the patients, they never stood a chance. In some cases this may actually have been true. A diagnosis of schizophrenia or bipolar somewhere in the family could in fact doom you. But even so, some found the strength and courage to get past it all—the pain, the shock, the trauma. Some people found ways to get through it. Why others can't, I couldn't tell you. I'm stumped. That's part of the reason I find myself here. I need an explanation, but all I have are more questions.

As I read through the criteria for depression in the *DSM*, staff and clients buzz around me, but no one seems to notice me sitting here. Even after someone bumps into me, then places a hand on my shoulder to acknowledge the thump, everyone keeps moving. No apology necessary.

I'm invisible here. The only time I really felt like I was seen was when I was asked on occasion, "How many more do you need to see?" This process had become so much like herding. Nameless animals with numbers attached to their ears roaming around from place to place waiting for the inevitable. They all had different travels, but in the end, for most of them, it was all the same. Some lost their bandages soon after leaving this place and quickly crash-landed in a hospital psych ward. Others cycled through here or places like it week after week getting their monthly dose of first aid, psych meds, and painkillers.

As I pretend to read further along the page, the silence is broken by an angry resident. This has become a twice-weekly tradition. Someone was always upset, and none of them ever knew why, like a three-year-old throwing a tantrum and looking for attention. Sadly, that's how they get treated. "Soft voice," I tell myself, "be calm." I walk through the halls as the crowd shies away. Unlike the real world, when things get crazy in here, everyone flees the scene. Someone is always uncomfortable, someone is always triggered, and someone is always ready to leave and needs to be talked into staying.

The situation is quickly resolved. We didn't even have to call the police or get Psychiatric Emergency Response Team (PERT for short) involved. That's a good night if there ever was one. I avoid the group of clients all gathered in the upstairs TV room. I have one and a half hours left in my shift and at least three hours of work to do. Back to the *DSM*. I flip it open right to the page discussing MDD and slide my finger along the sentences, making mental check marks in my head. I know what his diagnosis is. I've known from the moment he walked in, head hanging, eyes drooping. His sad demeanor was enough to make even me want to cry, and I don't cry. I hadn't had a really good cry in years. I tried making myself cry from time to time. I thought it would help clear my head and allow me to let go of some of the stress and baggage I'd been carrying around.

It was my therapist who pointed out to me during one of our forced encounters that I carried everyone else's responsibilities and burdens. I had a habit of making everyone else's problems my own. I liked her. I don't know why. I envisioned myself telling her every secret that I had tucked away for no one to see. There was something comforting about her that put me at ease. The only problem was that she was a therapist, just like me. She's not my friend, my confidante, or my go-to home girl from around the way. She is just a therapist. What we do is a job. We grab at whatever we can, build rapport, check a few boxes, and hope that the client can eventually solve his or her own problems. How sincere could she really be? My uncertainty couldn't let me speak. So for the first few weeks of our relationship, we mostly just sat. I was seeing her weekly to meet my mandatory personal growth hours. It was a school requirement for all doctoral students. They wanted us to get to know what it was like to be on the other side of the room, I guess. I gave her just enough of me to satisfactorily earn the money I was paying her. Somewhere along the line, things changed. When my thirty weeks were up, I wasn't ready to go. I still didn't want to talk about anything. But I didn't want to go.

I was sitting at my computer when he came to the door. "I'm finished eating," he said, "Do you mind if I have a smoke?' No, I said, go ahead. It amazed me when I initially began working here how these people, who were in crisis, homeless, down and out, always managed to have a cigarette. That's one of three things mentally ill patients always have access to. Most of them had no income at all, and the ones who did often spent it before it even cleared their accounts. And yet there were always cigarettes to go around.

He took his time getting through the door, stopping to say hello to the other residents and initiate several short conversations. He has no idea how much work I need to do. He doesn't care. None of them do. Most of them come in here with such an entitled attitude. It makes it hard for me to empathize with them. They think that we're all here for them. We are, but not in the ways that they want us to be. They want us to solve all their problems, make everything better. They come in expecting us to find them housing they can't afford, a job they won't be able to keep, and an endless surplus of money they haven't earned but believe that their disability entitles them to.

I'm on the verge of a break. I have everything I want, and I love my job. Really! I love working with the people who come through these doors, but some days, like today, I'd rather be anywhere but here. I'm back to reading the *DSM* while I wait, and I'm slowly realizing that it's my own diagnosis I'm looking for.

Something isn't right. I can't get out of bed, I'm not eating, I'm isolating myself, and the things I used to enjoy mean nothing to me. I want to scream. I want to cuss some folks out. I want to tell some people what the real problem here is and what I really think about them. But just like my will to climb onto my treadmill each day, my physical ability to do or say anything just isn't here. I can't bring myself to be happy or mad. And all of the so-called professionals, trained to catch something like this, don't even see me sitting here. No one has said a word to me in over forty minutes, and we're sitting in the same cramped room with too many chairs and too many people, as usual. I'm feeling claustrophobic, so I refuse to make eye contact with anyone. That way I can pretend that I'm all alone. I take a deep breath and continue sitting here, indifferent, trying to decipher my own tangled web of emotionlessness. Am I?

My mom and brother had both been given the diagnosis years before, and my little sister had her run-ins with it as well, but me? I've always had it together. No matter the catch of the day, I was ready. I always got my shit done, but today? Today I feel like I'm ready to break. I just don't have the energy to do it.

He Said, She Said, I Said

My body can't tell night from day. The fumes I'm running on are turning against me, poisoning me from the inside out. There's no pleasure in this life anymore. No joy in pretending this broken facade is good for anything. I push on anyway. These are the "for worse," moments we speak of when we take our vows. They'll soon pass. At least I hope they will because that's what I tell my clients in group therapy everyday.

My neck is sore and bears the bruises from when he grabbed me and pulled me down. He pulled my hair so hard that when he took his hand away, my hair went with it. I have a bald spot. The hair will eventually grow back, but I will always see that spot when I look at myself as the hair there grows thinner than it was before. I spent a week in a hotel after that. That's also where I celebrated my twenty-eighth birthday—alone. I came home to flowers and balloons. Another vase to add to the collection. There are thirteen now. I hate flowers. I fucking hate them. We're on good terms now, but I haven't figured out what it is that I do that makes him so upset. So I'm on eggshells.

"When are you going to start working out again?" he asks nonchalantly with his feet propped up on my ottoman. I bought that. I bought it with him and his endless soccer watching in mind. He should be comfortable after a long day of work. That was my job, my mission, to keep him comfortable. *Asshole!* I think. I dare not say it aloud. He's irritated, and I don't want to set him off again. Not tonight. We're barely on speaking terms as it is. He chased me two days ago. I ran into our bedroom, closed the door, and locked it before he reached me. He kicked it down. The crack on the door is a constant reminder of that terrifying moment. There's always this thought that today may be the day he goes just a little too far. I stood paralyzed in fear behind that door. It gave way, much too easily. I was still in my gym clothes. He knew I still ran. Everyday I ran. It was becoming clear that the direction I was running in was not the right one, however.

I'd become so used to being called other names that when he did use my real name, I often didn't realize he was talking to me unless he was looking me in the eyes. He hated me. Maybe not, but that's how he made me feel. But he also loved me. Maybe not in love, but I'd convinced myself he must at least like me. Right? He wouldn't come home at night, continue to sleep with me, to have sex with me, if he didn't at least like me. I was different, after all. That was what he said. I was mature, knew what I wanted—I was strong, independent, ambitious. I was what he wanted. His mother would be proud that he'd met someone like me—someone who could cook his meals, or at least try to, clean the home, make his bed, and pay his bills. I was what he wanted. That's what he said in his sexy islander accent. He married me, after all. He even argued with me, offended by my refusal to take his last name; which I eventually acquiesced and took. He was happy with me and wanted the world to know that I belonged to him. I was what he wanted and needed.

He was my friend. I could tell him everything. Never in a million years did I think he'd use my secrets, my own words, against me. The things I told him were now daggers aimed at my heart. He hurt my feelings. It was worse than any physical pain I'd ever bear. I was pathetic. I cried but stood my ground as he spit my own words back at me. Telling me I was fat, unattractive, full of myself, stuck up, a selfish snob. I was a loser, he said. "Your own family doesn't even like you."

Things escalated. He threw a pot of hot oil at me. I'd used that pot to cook his dinner only an hour earlier. It wasn't scalding hot anymore but warm enough to make my skin itch from the sting. "You bitch, I fucking hate you!" I knew he was just mad. He didn't hate me. When he calmed down, I knew he'd apologize; and he did. He always did.

"You just make me so mad sometimes," he says. "Of everyone I know, you just get under my skin for some reason. I don't act like this with anybody else. No one makes me as mad as you do." I'm a trigger for him, I realize. But tomorrow he'll tell me he loves me. He'll tell me I'm selfless, honest, one of a kind, and the best thing that's ever happened to him. He'll even thank me for putting up with someone like him for so long. He may even say it with a card if I'm lucky. He'll swear he'll never hurt me again. And even though he continues to break his promise, as I always do, I'll believe him. He can only get this emotional if he really cares about me, I tell myself. He just expects more from me. I've somehow let him down. It's my own damn fault. I was wrong, and I apologize. I always eventually do. He says he loves me. He says he still wants me. He says he needs me. And I choose to believe him.

"You're beautiful," she says. She's a colleague of mine here at the state hospital I now work at. I am now thirty-three-years-old. "You're so smart! I can't believe you're a doctor." And I'm officially embarrassed.

I don't know why, but compliments have never sat well with me. They're usually followed by, "Are you broke?" "Can I ask a favor of you?" "Hey, can you..." No one gives compliments freely. They always have strings attached. And people definitely don't say nice things about complete strangers. I mean, I know of her, and she knows of me, we've even spent time together outside of work, but we don't *know-know* each other. I don't understand why she is being so nice to me. She claims she is impressed by my intelligence and questions me about my upbringing. I give her half-truths, enough to give the appearance that I'm interested in continuing this game in which she lays it on thick before asking me to do something I have no desire to do but will lack the ability, common sense, and courage to say *hell, no* to.

She's pretty. Any man would be happy to be with her. Her arms are so much smaller than mine. Her voice, unlike mine, is feminine, sexy, and womanly. Her height is perfect. Mine? I'm too tall to be short and too short to be considered model tall. She's exotic. I don't know her true heritage, but every day I see her I imagine some, far-off location with clean air, clear water, and perfect weather where she grew up surrounded by beautiful people who adored her. I bet she has more friends than she can even keep up with.

What does she really want? Why is she here in my office being so nice? She likes my nappy curls. I don't use chemicals, so when my hair's not pressed, it's a community gathering of uneven crinkles, curls, and half-curls. Her hair is long and naturally curly too, but in a different way than mine. The texture says she may be mixed, but with what I can't quite figure out. How could she like hair like mine when hers is so goddamn dreamy? She's full of shit. What does she want? I'm being nice to her. I haven't asked her to leave yet. I bet she's popular and always has been. The last thing I want to do is offend her or get on her bad side. The last thing I need is to be bullied again, talked about aloud as if I'm deaf and can't hear the names they call me.

You can say I'm being presumptuous to assume there's a dislike for me behind her fake smile. I don't think I'm wrong though, because she said I'm beautiful. No one else has ever said that to me. Not even my husband. He said, "I don't date ugly chicks." That's as close as he ever got. So to say I'm beautiful implies that she's not being honest. She's so damn happy every time I see her. What the hell is there to smile about? I mean, we all have good days and bad days, but who the hell is happy every day? Liars are, I convince myself.

I like talking to her. She seems friendly, harmless, innocent, and maybe a bit naive. But why is she here? Here in my office telling me how much she admires me? How special I am. How rare it is to stand before someone as educated, as impressive, and as beautiful as me. I know I'm not beautiful, because if I were, he would have told me so. But she says I am, so I know she's lying. I know she can't be trusted. I have the same face, flat ass, invisible hips, black, chapped lips, and chunky thighs. My feet are too big, and I'm taller than most other women. Nothing about me has changed. She thinks I'm some mythical person who conquered all and rose to the top of the food chain, but I'm no different than I was yesterday. I'm still that bitch he fucking hated so goddamn much. She says I'm beautiful, and for a moment I pause with gratitude because I've never heard those words directed toward me before. But then reality kicks in, and the sound of her voice is like nails to a chalkboard, and I know she's lying because she said I'm beautiful and I know—no, I choose not to believe her.

"Things will get better," I tell them. I'm in a room full of angry teenagers. They're forced to be here by court order. Some of them will eventually let me in and tell me all about the abuse, the drugs, and the dysfunction that goes on in their homes, about how hard it is to focus on school when they're up all night listening to their parents fight or hungry because there was nothing to eat. Drugs gave them a sense of community, a camaraderie outsiders like me could never understand. They gave them a reason to be accepted by someone—anyone, and an out, a way to feel numb or get through whatever it is that teenagers need to get through.

I am their therapist, the neutral person in the room and in their lives who will show them all the options they have available, all the ways they can change the course of their lives before things get too far off track. I tell them ways to get their needs met and how to communicate with their parents and teachers so they no longer need drugs to get them through the day.

"Whatever, man. You don't know what it's like to be us." I disagree and begin to explain. Without disclosing my entire life, I give them enough to make me relatable. I tell them that life does get better and that I'm living proof. I've survived so much in my thirty years of life. Being a teenager doesn't last forever. I try to give them the tools they need to be better individuals. They don't see their court-ordered time with me as beneficial or necessary. They can't see past whatever person, place, or thing they are missing out on in order to be here.

The court order is just another way society keeps children like them in order, in their place. They can't—won't allow themselves to see this as an opportunity to make their lives better. All they see is a bunch of adults who don't understand them but insist on making decisions for them. Why won't they listen to me? Why don't they believe me? I'm the expert here. I can help them if they would just let me. But they don't trust me. I'm just another thorn in their sides, another wall in their way. Therapy is another restriction, consequence, and reason to go light up somewhere and get wasted.

Why won't they believe me? I have no reason to lie to them. I have nothing to gain by seeing them acquiesce. I want them to have backbones, to fight for what they believe in and want in life. I just want them to be safe while doing it. It's my job to convince them that they are all capable of greatness and can be whoever they want to be, go wherever they want to go, do whatever it is their hearts tell them to do.

"My friends had to see a shrink too," one boy says. "He said not to say anything because you're just going to turn it around on me and twist my words."

"I shouldn't be here. I'm not crazy," another one says. "Therapy is for crazy people." I've tried everything. My hat of tricks is empty. I could have the next president of the United States in this room with me tonight. The next superstar, MD, teacher—none of this matters if I can't convince them of this, and right now they don't believe a thing that comes out of my mouth.

"Your parents love you," I say. But they don't believe me. "The world is yours for the taking," I tell them. They call me a liar and accuse me of just saying anything and everything I think might get them off the drugs. They are convinced that their drug of choice helps them in ways my words never can or will. I can't make them feel smarter the way they claim they do when they're high on weed, can't make them feel numb the way they do after chewing on some hallucinogenic mushrooms. I can't take away the pain as sufficiently or as quickly as a forty-ounce malt liquor beverage can.

I can tell them how to survive this crazy time in their lives. But no matter what I say, they don't believe me. They won't listen. They believe everything their doped-out homies say, even though their words have no truth, substance, or meaning. They fail to see the conflict in receiving advice from people who benefit from having someone else around to point the finger at when things go wrong. I'm trying to save them, and they won't listen to a word I'm saying. For whatever reason, it benefits them to choose to listen to everyone else but me. I am the voice of reason, but I'm competing against people who fist fight for them, who supply them with drugs and alcohol, people who accepted them when no one else would. I can't compete with that.

I'm trying to save their lives, but I'm failing miserably. I don't understand why they can't see that I have nothing to gain by lying to them and I really do want the best for them. It's breaking my heart that I can't get through to them. I'm throwing out everything I can, but they're so entrenched in their ways, stuck in the not-so-comfortable comfort zone, afraid to give in to change, and fighting like hell against anything that challenges what they've built for themselves and have grown accustomed to. I'm giving it my all, going down the list of possible interventions because I'm desperate to save their lives. I know I can save them if they would just let me. But for some damn reason they just won't. They've made the choice before even setting foot in this room that no matter what I say or do, they just can't—no, *won't,* believe me.

Marked

Whoever it was who said men were simple creatures lied. The men I've experienced all defined themselves by their ability to control and possess. When you're in a relationship but as ambitious as I am, with no desire to be possessed, a battle of wills ensues, and it's not always a clean or fair fight. There's nothing simple about that.

I wasn't prepared for my husband or the man I dated just before him. Truth be told, they were one and the same. Ultimately, I ended my previous relationship and my marriage for the same reasons. Although my prior boyfriend wasn't physically abusive, he was controlling and obsessive, so much so that he scared me. When I found out years later that he'd been incarcerated for beating up his wife, resulting in her hospitalization, I thought I'd dodged a bullet.

I entered another relationship almost immediately, not realizing I was marked. I still am. Not just from my intimate relationships but my relationship with men in general, including my father. When you are victimized, cast aside, made to feel insignificant or devalued in any way, it changes you. You become branded with a mark that others will see and use against you. Your inability to easily trust, hard exterior, and determined independence are all things that Mr. Wrong will see as a challenge. He will look at you, at me, as something broken that he can piece together to his liking. He won't fix me in a manner that's necessary for my survival. He won't make me stronger. He will instead take every piece of me that he can get his hands on and build me into the person or object most fitting for his survival.

My husband knew what he was getting when he met me. I was honest from day one. I told him I didn't want children before we were even married. I told him I wanted to get my doctorate degree, even though I had barely obtained my associate's degree when we began dating. In couples therapy years later, our therapist asked my husband, "Did you just not believe her when she told you of her ambitions?"

He replied simply, "People talk." Apparently he never believed I was as determined as I actually was or that I really meant it when I said I had no intention of getting pregnant by him or anyone else, ever. He complained that I wasn't submissive enough and that I didn't need him. When I saw something I liked or wanted, I didn't give him a chance to get it for me or surprise me. That I totally missed the fact that all men want to feel wanted. Even more than that, all men need to be needed. He didn't think I needed him, and he desperately wanted to be needed. That's what ultimately destroyed our home.

My superhero costume was cami-green. I was seventeen when I enlisted. I will meet my husband in two years while stationed in California. He was a marine as well. When I suited up each day, I felt a physical transformation occur. The honor of being part of a team that protected not only those I loved but others I'd never know was unexplainable. I always left home with my head held high. It is an indescribable and immeasurable feeling that I value to this day. It gave my life purpose. It gave my struggles meaning. To be part of my country's watch gave me fulfillment. I find that same fulfillment each day I show up at work and oversee the transformations of my patients. There is no greater feeling than the one I get when I am helping others. That's why I was so disappointed when my superiors turned their backs on me.

They, my command, ignored my pleas for help and my request mast; a filing of a formal complaint. I had filed it against a male colleague I worked with who outranked me by one grade. They chose instead to handle matters in-house, closing ranks to protect the US Marine Corps' pride and joy—the men. My abusive relationships with men didn't start when I married. They began long before then. I was surrounded by trained killers and some of the craziest people I knew, but sharing a bond, a camaraderie with them made me feel like I was in the safest place on earth when in their presence. I was slapped, gripped by my arms, slammed against walls, and drunk-dialed by my male superior on several occasions. I endured because I was a WM. That was an abbreviation for woman marine but also stood for waste management because a female marine could have semen deposited inside of her, at times leading to pregnancy. Male marines who slept around avoided this condition courtesy of their anatomy.

I was a good marine, and I did my job well. I knew I was entering a world not meant for me, but I wanted the challenge, and I thought I'd earn the respect of the men I was surrounded by. I fit in with them. Not quite a tomboy, but definitely not a girly girl, I was one of the guys, and I loved it. Here my looks or lack thereof, my family life, how much money I did or didn't have, my many imperfections—they didn't mean a thing. My job was to make my command, its officers, and my officer in charge look good and follow the code: God, country, corps. There was no right or wrong. No such thing as injustice—just the code.

I understood the code. I even respected it. Still do. It was an unspoken understanding. It included keeping our business to ourselves. I was raised to never discuss family business outside of our home, so it made sense to not advertise my command's inability to control one of its own, which would no doubt be embarrassing, especially considering everything else going on in the world after September 11. Complaining about things, I feared, would make me no more than the lazy, thin-skinned, crybabies my supervisors thought most females were. I was never shielded from the true feelings most of my male counterparts held. We were liabilities in every sense of the word; we were weak, obnoxious, boy-crazed, less intelligent, less capable, and—most important—a distraction.

Whether I agreed with it or not, I always knew that if it came down to it, my duty was to place the needs of the corps before my own. There was no way I could ever bring shame to this institution, even if that meant being shamed by it.

I worked hard and managed to create a good name for myself. But unlike the men I served with, I had to prove myself everyday, all over again. I knew the first thing people saw when I entered a room was a black person. I was a woman second and a marine third. Because of this I worked twice as hard as some of my male colleagues even though I received little to no recognition from those from whom it mattered most. I loved my time in the corps, but that didn't change the fact that every day was my first day in my male superiors' eyes. My experience regarding the abuse I suffered was troublesome and difficult to process alone, which was what I was forced to do. Even so, the bad times during my tour of duty were far fewer than the good times, and my experience overall was a good one and something I wouldn't trade for the world. This didn't change the fact that I was not a valued member of the team and that I was once again made to feel dispensable.

I just started working here a few months ago having finally completed graduate school at thirty-two-years-old. I'm in my program director's office. He is behind his desk asking me a question. My supervisor is sitting to my right. He blocks me from the door, my only escape. I am not afraid. At least that's what I keep telling myself. To my surprise I actually like my program director. I only believe about fifty percent of what he says to me, but this could be for many reasons, mostly having to do with my own journey, and does not necessarily correlate to his true level of integrity.

My supervisor, on the other hand, freaks me out a bit, a fact I chose not to keep from him. He exudes referent and expert power over me that elicits both fear and respect from me. In the short time we have worked together he has somehow mastered the unsettling ability to simultaneously unnerve and steady me. Because of the impact he has on me he is the most dangerous. Although he doesn't have my complete trust, I trust him the most. He could hurt me by breaking that trust easier than anyone else and—if our past is any predictor of our future—he will. Although he is often stoic and hard to read, and has an annoying habit of popping up at my office unannounced, he appears to be sincere.

I am calm. I learned long before starting this job to feign a toughness that is nowhere close to my true psychological state. A lack of working collaboration among my heart, mind, and body often left me disconcerted and in a state of complete indecisiveness. This internal discord left me in constant disarray. Even so, I was often, for the most part, able to maintain my composure. My stubborn refusal to give in or settle, my ability to hide what I was really thinking and feeling, and the way I was always able to compartmentalize would soon be defined as resilience and dedication and some of the many reasons I'm still standing today. Or so I've told myself.

The truth is I am terrified to be in the presence of authority figures. I always fear they will abuse their power over me somehow. This is especially so for most men who have some authority over me. Long before they give me a reason to like or dislike them, I struggle to trust them because of the pieces of my past they represent. When I am with my administrative supervisor, however, I sense his warm spirit and am often comforted.

Although he can be a straight shooter, a man of few words leaving lots to the imagination, who doesn't necessarily say what I want him to say, he does his job well from what I can tell, and I respect him. Because of this, I do my job as well as I possibly can. I correlate my respect for him with my ability to stay out of trouble and not draw any unnecessary attention his way.

At some point our casual conversation goes south. I'm not sure why, but I am increasingly panicked. I can feel my breath catching as I attempt to stop myself from wheezing aloud. I am taking deeper than usual breaths, trying to steady my nerves. I feel claustrophobic suddenly, and I want to leave but am embarrassed by the thought of how stupid I'd look if I just got up and walked out. This panics me even more. I want to leave, but I can't. But I also can't stay.

My hearing is fading. Although I see his lips moving as he leans over his desk, I can't hear a word he's saying to me. I begin staring at his lips in a desperate attempt to read his words and force a response if necessary. This is something I've often done during similar episodes. My supervisor, clearly on my side, has momentarily become my enemy. He is keeping me from excusing myself. I can't see past him at the moment.

The door is only a few feet to his right, but at the moment it might as well be miles away. I feel like I am going to faint. I am so appreciative of the seat beneath me. At least my fall won't be too far. I'm also comforted by the fact that I'm wearing my new Victoria's Secret underwear. Ever since my brother's death, I've had a fear that if I ever fainted in public, my clothes would be cut off in a desperate attempt to save my life, a fact only solidified by my time in the military, where fainting meant a date with the silver bullet—a thermometer shoved up one's ass in order to gauge body temperature to check for heatstroke.

I am overwhelmed by my attempts to read the program director's lips, steady my breathing so that I don't pass out, dry my sweaty hands against my pant legs, bite my lips to keep them from quivering and plan my escape from this hell. I can hear my heart beating in my ears as the room begins to blur and time begins to fade. I am suddenly asked to leave.

It's not until sometime later, when my supervisor asks me if I'm feeling better, that I realize that my discomfort must have been obvious. In the past it was the sudden change in my body temperature that alerted me to an impending panic attack. I usually had time to go hide or calm myself down. Neither of the latter were options. For now however, as I sit in my supervisors office, as quickly as it started, no longer caged between two powerful men, it was over, and I was strong again.

Enough?

Lunatics, whack jobs, crazies, schizos, weirdos, bums, manipulators, monsters, tards, psychos—aka the mentally ill. I thought I'd heard it all. Boy, was I wrong.

"How did you become such an ass?"

Without hesitation I respond, "Years of hurt." I'm not sure what surprised me more, her question or my response. It was as if I had been prepped and ready for someone to question me so offensively for some time. She, a good friend of mine who had joined me for dinner, laughs—it's a joke. But I know that there's some truth behind the words. If this is my response, my reason for having such a shitty attitude all the time, then things are worse than I had ever imagined. People around me have begun to accept that this is just who I am; a mean, judgmental, moody, short-tempered, impatient, arrogant, and, like the governess from *The Sound of Music*, far too outspoken individual.

How could I have taken everything I've experienced over the past decade and turned it into something so unjust, unfitting, and unbecoming and directed it toward others? Had I not learned anything? I am my worst fear and my biggest pet peeve—a hypocrite. I'm shocked and disappointed in myself. My good days far outweighed the bad ones, but the bad ones were pretty rough. I told myself years ago that I wouldn't become the thing that I despised so much in others and that I'd use optimism to get me through each trial. I had seen, heard, and felt so much discomfort and disappointment. I wouldn't wish it on anyone else. They were supposed to make me stronger. I pray it was not for nothing.

Working as a therapist takes so much out of me sometimes. I am empathetic, understanding, patient, open-minded, and sincere on most days. I pour myself into my work. Not just because I'm good at it, but because my work is a direct reflection of who I am and those who have trained and mentored me.

I want the clients, patients, and offenders to be better people, to be able to have something to look forward to, something better than what they've experienced thus far. I want them to have the lives that they deserve even if they don't feel worthy. I want them to accept and be okay with who they are and the things they've been through and learn from their past troubles instead of hiding and trying to evade them. I want to teach them how to be products not of their circumstances but of their positive choices. I want the same thing for them that I want for myself. It bothers me so much how people can survive the craziest, scariest, and most trying catastrophes like molestation, the death of a child, heartbreak, cancer, and other unimaginable traumas and then crawl into an invisible hole and choose to stay there, or worse, do to others what they themselves struggled through, feared, and barely escaped.

Nothing we do going forward can change the past. Even I have to remind myself of this. How is surviving trauma in itself not enough to shock anyone into action, to motivate them to fight back by being better and stronger than before? When you hurt so bad that you don't want to go on, it seems that it would be easy to just say to yourself, *Tomorrow has to be better.* No one really knows, but sometimes a lie is much better than sitting in sorrow.

I lie to myself every day. I'm good at it. Maybe this is partly why depressed people bother me so much. I can't lie to them. They can see straight through me. They very rarely believe me. I realized a while ago that I can relate to depressed clients far more than any other client who has sat and possibly ever will sit across from me. It's hard to look in the mirror sometimes. It's even harder to accept that this may be as good as it gets. How can I accept that? How can anyone accept that? How can I learn to live with just good enough? How can I teach others that this may be as a good as it gets and that they too must learn to cope with just good enough, that no matter how much effort they put forth, this is as good as life gets and they are the best that they may ever be? Maybe that's why I'm so damn angry. Maybe my good enough just isn't enough.

I'm at dinner with my girlfriends when one of them jokingly calls me stupid. I instantly respond by calling her retarded. We carry on with our laughs, inappropriate comments, and dinner. We don't think twice about the names we are calling one another. We don't, for one moment, pause to challenge our poor choice of words to describe one another. It's all in fun, so there's no harm in it. I've made inappropriate comments before.

Hell, I am a walking microphone without a filter. I am typically heard long before I am seen and often memorable to people that I meet for all the wrong reasons. I once called a woman a cunt. I yelled it from my car window after she stole a parking spot that I had been patiently waiting for outside the busiest Costco in the world on a hot-ass Saturday morning. I felt justified. Stealing parking spots is a serious offense! When I slipped up and called someone I barely knew a cunt a few years later, I was horrified. Call it a Freudian slip or just plain stupidity—either way, I was embarrassed. I had embarrassed myself and I wanted to take it back immediately, but the damage was done. It got me thinking. How the hell could you make such a huge blunder, and in public? I had become so used to being inappropriate, speaking before thinking, not filtering, that all the positives in my life were being overshadowed by the mean and nasty things I had done and was continuing to do.

I don't like who I've become. I am judgmental. I lack tolerance. I don't play nice with others. I am not open or welcoming to people and things that I do not understand or want to deal with. I do not like change. I do not like to be challenged. Although I am a fiercely loyal friend, I am just as passionate at being your worst enemy. I'm like a betta. It's a beautiful fish, but it has to live in a world by itself because of its temperament and inability to socialize. But every day I get up, I dress myself, I ready myself, and I go out into the world, and I lie. I lie to myself, and I lie to everyone around me. I do and say whatever I need to in order to make it through the day. When I come home at night, I pace the floor and lie awake disappointed in myself. I spend hours reminiscing about my day. And without sleep, I get up, and I do it all over again. Who the hell am I to tell people that they need to work on themselves if I can't even work on me?

I'm at camp. Black people don't camp. When you grow up fighting to not be homeless, you don't wake up one day and decide to pretend to be. Add my disliking for dirt, spiders, bugs, sleeping outdoors, not having cell reception, having to share a shower, waking up early, being somewhere I can't find my way back from without a GPS or compass, my social anxiety, being surrounded by teenagers, being outnumbered by teenagers, being outnumbered by spiders and bugs, buffet-style meals, no privacy—did I say spiders and bugs? Yeah, camping just wasn't my thing. It was supposed to be an opportunity to positively impact the lives of the youth in our presence, to lead by example and influence healthy lifestyle choices.

When a discussion about the n-word came up, initially I was dismissive, but as the conversation continued, as usual, something or someone drew me in.

When a young Caucasian male from the audience asks the group of African-American students standing on stage as part of an activity about cultural acceptance, inclusiveness, openness, and many other things that I would fail miserably at trying to describe in a few sentences, if he could use the n-word, the answer he gets is, "Hell, no," and everyone laughs. He says it jokingly, but we all know he means it. In no way, shape, or form or in any period of time in this or any other lifetime would it be acceptable for a white kid to call someone who is black a nigger. No matter how street the white person thought he or she was or how thugged out, hip, gangsta, or froggy they were feeling, this is just inappropriate and could get a person rocked—knocked the fuck out. No matter what letters you put at the end, changing the *er* to an *a*, it's the same word.

I'm standing with these students, and I agree that the use of the infamous F word is unacceptable, but there's a conflict here, at least for me. So I speak up. I say that I agree that the word referenced above should not be spoken. That its origins are unforgettable and remain attached to it each time it is used. That no matter how much you try to fancy or change it up, the word remains the same and is highly offensive. But more important, and probably most shocking, we, the group of thirty or so black staff and students onstage, have no right to tell people like the young man in the audience that they cannot use it simply because they are not black. Instead, he should continue to use it because we ourselves do. No matter who it comes from, at the end of the day, it's the same word with the same meaning. We, black people, use it all the time and throw it around, disregarding its offensively derogatory nature, and until we police ourselves and stop using it, we lose the right to tell others that using it is wrong. I don't know why I spoke up, or where my words came from, but I meant them. Maybe it's because I hate hypocrites. Maybe it's because I thought that my silence would make it appear as if I were in agreement with the exchange between the two students.

There I go again, being a hypocrite. Although I'd never use the n-word, there are many just as offensive words that I still use every day. I get mad when I hear others speak poorly about the mentally ill. It makes my blood boil, and I am instantly on the defense. But how can I be mad; really? I have so many flaws that I ignore. I am the last person who should be telling anyone that they need to be doing things differently.

In all honesty, I use up the best of me at work. By the time I get home, I'm exhausted. There's nothing left to work on myself. And continuously focusing on others allows me to avoid addressing my own shortcomings. To focus on me would mean that I would have to on some level acknowledge that I am imperfect and may always be. I struggle to get out of bed sometimes. I hate being around other people, partly because I have social anxiety, but also because I just don't care enough or have the energy to be casual and sociable with anyone. I project onto others the things that I think I should be feeling. Acknowledging myself would mean admitting that I am, on more days than not, unwell. My secrets, the things that I lie to myself and others about, haunt me. I know what's wrong with me. I am like a functioning alcoholic. I can't even say the word. I have moments when I am compelled to care, but this is not the case on most days. Not after a long day at work, anyway. And so I lie— whatever it takes to get through the day.

Tomorrow I will still be lying to myself, my friends will still call me stupid, and I will call them retards. And black people and white people alike will still use the n-word. I, like everyone else, am not ready for things to be any different than they are right now. So there's the answer to the question. I guess at this point in time, my life, and everything in it, is good enough.

Save Me

I like being in the dark. I don't why. I tell myself that it's because I can hide there. I'm running for my life. All I have is the dark. Every time I think I've found a dark, protective place to hide, the truth catches up with me. I know I'm strong, but lately I've questioned the fight in me. I don't know if my fragile strength is enough anymore. I'm beginning to think that it's time to turn and face the facts, one being that maybe I like the darkness not because it's a good place to hide from others but because I can try to hide from myself there. This is going to be harder than I ever imagined. I'm ready to stop running, to save myself, but I don't know if I can do this alone. I need a hero.

Everyone wants to be saved. We've all, at some time or another, fantasized about what our superhero would look like, how we would feel in the moment we realized we had been rescued and everything from that point on would be different, better somehow. But it's getting hard to imagine a world where heroes actually exist. The only ones left are on television. I want to believe that the American Dream, true love, harmony, and all the other things that fairy tales and childhood hopes are made of still exist, but I can't.

My house has been filled with people who have constantly lied to my face, used me, and said yes when they should have said no. I work with people who have victimized others, some repeatedly. Murderers, thieves, addicts, master manipulators. I'd like to say that they were all behind bars. The truth is some of them have passed security checks and been given uniforms. Some greet me with a smile every morning and call themselves my friends. And some share the same blood that I do.

I don't know up from down most days. It's not always clear who I should trust. I don't even trust my own judgment anymore. My confidence on most days has been long since depleted before I even get to my desk. They say that you can't work where I work without a healthy dose of fear. Well, you also can't walk down the streets where I live at night without a healthy dose of fear. If I am vulnerable at home around my own family and always looking over my shoulder at work, then where am I safe? I need some normalcy in my life. I want to feel safe. I want to be safe. I want to feel secure and protected. I want my childhood hope back. Where's that hero?

It's the year before I began working at the state hospital. I am completing my last years of training at a prison on the east coast. I work with rapists. One of my greatest fears in life is to be sexually assaulted. The only thing worse than being sexually assaulted is being sexually assaulted and given an incurable disease. Yet I go to work every day, and I look fear in the eyes. I couldn't tell you what a sex offender looks like, but if I walked past a few of these guys on the street or in the grocery store, I wouldn't think twice about them. They could have been college friends of mine, friends of my grandparents or parents, neighbors. I'm trying to rectify my ill feelings about the men who sit in front of and beside me in group therapy. I want to be able to work with these men the same way that I work with other clients. I want to give them the best of what I have to offer as a clinician. But after listening to them describe their crimes in detail, which is part of their treatment, I'm angry. I want to find something in common with them, something that's relatable. I really do. I'm really trying, but I can't get past my fear, my discomfort, and my disgust.

My second year practicum assignment was a crisis house. As I sat in the office waiting for instructions, a clinician walked in with a man and asked him to sit down. Without warning the clinician asked me to keep an eye on the man while she ran to speak to the nurse about his medications. Just the fact that he needed an eye on him made me uncomfortable, not to mention the fact that he also needed medicating. When he started talking to me, I thought something wasn't right with him. I was instantly on guard. He was upset because he couldn't reach his mom at the number on a little piece of paper he was holding. He curled himself forward and began rocking in his seat and speaking to himself. I watched him display several symptoms of psychosis, including paranoia. I'd read about this in school but had never seen it in real life. On one hand, I was excited that I was getting to experience this; however, there was also something extremely intimidating about witnessing my first real-life psychotic episode.

I sat as still as I could, keeping my eye on him so that the second he moved from his seat, I could make my escape out the office door. I didn't feel safe. I wanted to be here, and I wanted to work with people like him, but this was far more than I had bargained for. All the years I'd spent preparing for this, and I froze in the moment. I wanted to help people, but I was never really sure what helping people would look like. I'd been so emotionally disconnected over the past few years, unable to trust, unwilling to love, incapable of genuine, everyday, in-the-moment emotional expression. And yet here I was, scared to death and realizing that I needed to react but unable to. I had never wished so hard to be invisible. I didn't know what to expect. All I knew was that I was stuck in a room with a crazy person, and he was much closer to the door than I was. I was going to have to somehow get past him to make my escape if he lost it anymore than he already had.

I was a ball of emotions, with fear being the most recognizable one. The fact that I was able to recognize that I was scared terrified me even more. I hadn't cared enough to be afraid of anything in a long time. If something hurt or bothered me, I just shut it out of my life and never looked back. But I knew that if I couldn't make it through my first day in this crisis house, I would never be able to convince myself to come back. Effectively ending my mental health career before it could even began.

My personal life was chaos. I struggled with family life. I didn't like my husband. I had realized long before now that I was a dead zone. I had become extremely uninterested in sharing my life with anyone, including my friends. I had found a way to minimize the chaos and irritation that I was experiencing—a way to eliminate disappointment and keep the peace in my house, in my life, and in my mind. Over the years I had fallen into a role. Because of my consistency, people had become reliant on me in ways that I wasn't comfortable with. I had become predictable.

I learned during my time in the military that predictability leads to expectation, and expectation can lead to a lack of attention to detail. I was expected to accept things, to go along with things, to put up with things. I was a silent partner in my own life, and the details no longer mattered. If someone's feelings were hurt or I was clearly being used and taken advantage of, those were details that no one, including me, cared about. As long as everyone was outwardly happy and getting what they wanted, and no one was fighting or arguing, the fact that I was constantly doing things that went against my own personal morals and beliefs and sitting silent when I should have spoken up for myself and others didn't matter.

I shut myself down. I became a robot, just going through the motions. Deep down I am frozen, and my attitude reflected every chunk of ice I carried. Although my newfound and accepted way of functioning was working for me at home, at work, and other places where contact with others wasn't a priority, I found that it didn't quite work the same in therapy.

I was a business owner. At the child-care center and after school program I opened at the age of twenty-three, I was able to distance myself from my employees and the everyday things that would drive the average person crazy: bickering, jealousy, envy, gossip. I don't care about how your weekend went, who got dumped, who got engaged, who had a baby—who cares? As an employee and part of a team, this was almost impossible to do. My personal life was impacting my ability to be a great clinician and team player before I had even begun my career.

I had to figure out how to revive myself, but just enough to be able to work effectively, without exposing myself to the same ailments and pernicious people and things that I had been hiding from all these years. How I was going to do this was a mystery. I had been so disconnected for so long that the on switch was rusted out. It wasn't as simple as just making a decision and going with it. I had to take steps that I wasn't ready or willing to take. I knew that something had to give, but what? There was no one that I could turn to about this. I didn't trust anyone enough to share what I was going through.

I had found pseudo-peace at home and pseudo-relationships with my friends but was now struggling at work for the first time ever, which brought back feelings of inadequacy. I had all the tools that I needed but wasn't applying them in any way that made sense, not even to me. I found a way to survive, but just surviving was beginning to no longer be enough. And I know the only one who can fix this, the only one who can turn it all around and save me, is me. I'm the hero I've been waiting for. If things were going to change, I was going to have to be my own savior. Saving others, I can do. Saving myself, that's another story.

For what felt like an eternity, I sat and stared. I didn't move, I didn't make eye contact, and I tried to make my breathing shallow so that I was as quiet as I could possibly be, which was becoming more and more difficult because my nervousness had caused my asthma to start acting up. Eventually the man began to calm himself down. He began telling himself that he was okay, that his mother was okay. He told himself that he should take a PRN, prescribed medication that patients are allowed to ask for and take when they feel they need it in order to decrease their symptoms. He looked at me. I was curious about what he was going to say and do next. He had my attention, and my interest was piqued. The therapist in training had awakened. As he introduced himself, I told myself, "You can do this; he's just like every other client you've worked with, except that he's in a crisis house, in crisis, medicated, paranoid, upset, and blocking the door."

He continued, "I've never seen you before. Nice to meet you; my name is…" Before I knew it, we had struck up a conversation. He was intelligent, which didn't make sense because I'd grown up believing that crazy people couldn't think straight and were messed up in the head.

And even though I'd been taught different in school I hadn't yet been able to see it for myself. I learned that he had a family, a life, and a daily routine. He'd even had a part-time job before coming here. We had more in common than I would have ever guessed. Finding something that I could relate to him about was much easier than I had thought it would be. Maybe it was my fear that had kept me from being able to see this sooner.

When I left that day, I remember thinking, *Hmm, I can't believe how normal that crazy man was.*

That was it—human. They are all human. Although I had fallen into a routine and was beginning to really enjoy my internship I was still struggling with feelings associated with working with sex offenders. As usual, I was in my head, barely paying attention to what was going on around me. There was a lot of discussion going on, a lot of back and forth, but I was more focused on my visual observations. I was taking in the faces of the men around me, looking for something that I could use to help me rationalize why I was in a room surrounded by criminals.

I was drawn into the conversation. They had fears, hurt, pain, and disappointments. They'd been let down and admittedly let others down.

They were hurting. Each and every one of them was going through his own personal struggle whether he realized it or not. And I could relate to that. I can't ever relate to being a sex offender, nor can I wrap my head around some of these guys' rationale for the crimes they'd committed, but under it all they were men. Without minimizing their crimes, I had somehow found that one thing my teacher used to tell us as students to look for—something you can relate to. I'd had some of the very same desires that these men were discussing. Wanting to be loved, respected, and needed, wanting to be accepted by family, to have job security, wanting to feel important, to have a sense of purpose. I'd shared a lot of the same fears. In a lot of ways we were different, but there were many similarities under it all.

My immediate thought was that I must be pretty fucked up to be able to relate to anyone in that room. I was disgusted with myself for looking at these offenders as human. Although I am enlightened to my own desires to be a people pleaser, accepted by others, appreciated and valued by my friends and those with whom I surround myself, and although it is hard to sympathize with people when they don't make good choices, the fact is that I do empathize with some of them. I feel sorry for them all. I feel sorry for myself. And I am embarrassed that I do. I empathize with each and every one of these men for different reasons. And I am shocked by my ability to humanize men who have, in my eyes, done some of the most inhumane things.

I am scared, afraid that something is wrong with me. I'm concerned because after all these years of deliberately feeling nothing, avoiding emotional exchanges, and giving nothing that would emotionally connect me to anyone, I have made a conscious decision to feel something here in this room. I am forever changed by this. I am changed because I know that the work, not with these men but on myself, will finally begin and that progress can finally be made. I know that I can't be a good therapist and help others until I can first help myself. Being able to look at myself as a human first—not a therapist, a daughter, a good or bad friend, a sister, winner, loser, or failure, but as nothing more than a human being with needs, wants, and desires makes change possible.

I recognize that there is nothing beneficial in being aware of the things that frighten me or make me uncomfortable if I am not willing to do something constructive about them. That's what therapy is all about. I had assumptions about what it meant to be mentally ill or a sex offender. The title "sex offender" implies a physical assault has taken place, when in fact the term encompasses an array of offenses from urinating in public and being a peeping Tom to other nonphysical as well as physical offenses. And being mentally ill doesn't mean that you're stupid or dangerous. My assumptions were wrong.

I don't know if this field chose me or if I chose it, but I'm here because I believe that people can change and that there is good in most of us. I came into this field to advocate for those who cannot advocate for themselves and educate myself and my community. Where and how I grew up has deeply influenced my beliefs, my morals, and my values. At some point, however, I have to decide how much of my past I want to retain. My values ten years ago are not the same as they are today, and my cultural belief system has been upgraded to include my current values and beliefs, which are based on my personal experiences. This is part of the struggle of working in this field—constantly coming into contact with others whose own belief systems don't mesh with your own and being able to work around that.

I like to use a weird laundry analogy that I made up a few years ago. Therapy is like being in a laundromat on a Saturday afternoon with tons of other people. You have to help everyone sort through all their belongings while sorting through your own crap at the same time. The trick is to get it done without mixing up all your belongings with anyone else's. It's easy to separate the things that don't look alike, but sometimes you find something in the pile of stuff that could just as easily belong to you. Transference, counter-transference, burnout—it's hard at first, but I've learned that sorting it all out does get easier. You just have to be willing to do the work.

I was taught that good therapists can help change the lives of others. A great therapist; however, is changed by the people they come in contact with. A great therapist can not only impact others but is always working on becoming a better individual. They recognize and accept that they are a work in progress. I am a work in progress. I've learned so much about myself in my short time working in this field. More important, I've learned that it's when I am the most uncomfortable or vulnerable that I am opening myself up to receive something really great.

If being able to relate to the mentally ill or sex offenders is an indicator of my own personal growth, then I don't think it's a bad thing. I can't be my best at work without being willing to continuously work on myself as well. I think I've finally found my hero. It's a team effort, but I think I'm ready to do my part. I'm ready to save myself.

Insanity

There is a fly skinny-dipping in my glass. Even more disconcerting is Celexa, my seven-month-old black Lab, who is running in circles in front of me. She's chasing her tail. I think she really believes that if she just keeps running in circles, she'll catch up to it one day. I am amazed by her stupidity, amused by her ability to keep busy by running in circles, barking at her own reflection in the TV screen—just doing random, stupid shit for hours at a time. *She gets this from her father's side of the family,* I tell myself. And that stupid fly. How many times will flies attempt to drink from glasses before they realize it will only lead to one thing—drowning? This fly cannot be that thirsty.

It's hard to watch the fly and Celexa and not think of all the stupid things that I've done to myself and others when people were watching, and even when I didn't think anyone was watching. I do it mainly out of boredom, anger, and disappointment, and almost always impulsively. I'm often left with that feeling in my gut: *Did you really just say or do that? Just slowly turn and walk away and don't look back, you're such a fucking idiot.* I also get laughed at fairly often. Now that I think about it, when compared to half the things I've done, Celexa's idiotic entertainment isn't so stupid after all. On a separate note, what does my amusement and time-consuming process of watching her say about me?

I love my baby sister. Although she is grown, she is still a baby to me. She is as much part of my life as anything or anyone I come into contact with on a daily basis. She's going to die. She tells me she wants to die. I talk her out of it. She gets better for a while, but she always calls back wanting to die. My heart tells me she's going to do it. She has her entire life to look forward to, but she can't see past today. She doesn't understand what our brother's death did to us all, how it destroyed this family. She was far too young to know what was going on at that time. And yet here she is, putting me through it all over again. She's sad, and because she's sad, she can't see how selfish she is being. I feel selfish for making this about me, but it is about me. I can't stand by and watch her die, but I love her too much to cut her loose. She'll make the decision she wants to make with or without my permission.

Although her decision will ultimately be about her, I feel like it's about me not being strong enough for the both of us, me not having the right words or giving the right support—whatever that may be. Her life is not what she wants it to be. She comes to me, and I don't know what to say. I don't know what she expects from me. Maybe it's because I'm the psychologist in the family. Maybe it's because she is the closest to me and trusts me the most. Maybe she is hoping I will say something that will make it better. I often feel like she is depending on me to take her pain away and save her life. When I don't hear from her, I worry. I wish I were closer to her and not hundreds of miles away. But I am also secretly relieved that I am hundreds of miles away. I don't want to find her body. I don't want to have to do CPR again. I don't want to have to attend another funeral.

My life has always been about contrast. Behaving like a white girl or valley girl, even though I am pretty sure I am anything but and still don't even know for sure exactly what this means, as opposed to the black girl I was born and raised to be. Growing up in one place with my mom and siblings and another with my dad and his family. Not being girly or submissive enough to keep a man or fit into my culturally assigned role. Being too independent and strong-willed, but too weak and sensitive to truly be considered one of the guys. Not standing up for myself and being too passive while also being accused of being too direct and assertive—for a girl.

I apparently also dress too street and not professional enough, as if this makes me less intelligent or less worthy of someone's respect. And I've been accused of wearing my hair natural only to prove that I'm black enough to retain my *black* card and accused of being a traitor or not comfortable in my own skin for pressing it straight or wearing a weave.

I've struggled for years to find my own identity. It's hard to develop a sense of self and identity when everywhere you go you're always being compared to someone or something or held to someone else's expectations of who you should be. When your life is defined by a plethora of labels others have chosen for you without any consideration for your own desires, fitting in is rough.

I began operating from a position of detachment and insularity. When I was tired, stressed, lonely, depressed, or down on myself, which was true on more days than not, a proclivity for hard work kicked in, becoming my salvation and what got me through each moment and ultimately each day. Whatever I could do to keep busy was what I did. Work became my distraction, and I, like Celexa, chased my tail a lot trying to make everyone around me happy.

Work, home. Work, home. Work, home. This was my everyday routine. Because being around normal people made me feel crazy and overwhelmed, I decided that spending as much time as possible with people who, for lack of a better choice of words were deemed crazy, would be my way of feeling somewhat normal. I'd learned how to hide my weaknesses behind my strengths and the flaws of others years ago. On the East Coast, you had to be strong. Anything less marked you as prey. I don't want to be prey, at least not anymore.

"Forty" is beautiful. That's the nickname I use for her. It represents a forty-ounce malt liquor bottle, traditionally served in a brown paper bag and symbolic of the East Coast, where she lives. She nicknamed me Canelli, which is the name of my favorite wine, representing the West Coast, where I live. She is smart, funny, and much stronger than she knows. She has so much going for her, but in the midst of her pain, like most of my depressed clients, she sees none of this. I am supposed to fix her. That's why she calls me. But as with so many other things in my life, I don't know how.

No matter how well things are going for me, every time she says she wants to die, the one thing I am the most proud and passionate about in this world, my work as a psychologist, means nothing. I feel like a failure. I can't enjoy my life because I am constantly worrying about hers and the impact the loss of it will have on me and everyone else around me. I can't sleep because of her. She's not the only reason, but she adds to my inability to be normal.

She refuses professional help, but she calls me. I'm a professional, but I don't know what to do. I am too close to her to treat her as a client. A client I could leave at work. She stays with me. I wait for the call and wonder where I will be and what I will be doing, whether I will be alone or surrounded by colleagues or friends. Will I attend her funeral and tend to the needs of her children? Will I be able to handle my mother's breakdown, which is sure to kill her too? My mother cannot handle another loss. I can't handle another loss. I cannot do this again. I can't survive another sibling's death.

I often wonder when I am standing between the security gates at work waiting for some invisible person whose job it is to push a button to let me in or out of the facility—who, might I add, always takes just a little too damn long, especially on cold and rainy days. Just push the damn button already! There must be something insane about the people who work here. Who in their right mind would allow the government to lock them in a building with people the government is too afraid to let walk the streets? There is something not right about all of us. This leads me to believe that some of my colleagues are probably just as crazy as the patients and prisoners I work with— maybe even crazier. And I sit in offices with them by myself and get in their cars. That makes me equally insane.

The fact is that we all have some level of psychosis that drives us. Even when not reaching clinical levels, we can be motivated by both good and evil or psychosis and baseline behaviors.

Baseline meaning behaviors that represent a balance of both socially acceptable behaviors and behaviors and norms typical of us individually. Maintaining some level of normalcy and being able to function without others noticing the crazy in us is what separates the undiagnosed and the why-the-hell-aren't-they-diagnosed from one another.

If we were to consider that I, a professional, person of reason and great problem-solving skills, have done some pretty unthinkable things, like slipping laxatives into someone's food thirty minutes prior to them leaving to board a seven-hour flight, but have also taken the shoes off my feet and given them to a young girl I met at a camp who needed them and just happened to wear my size, I think the possibility of crazy is clearly evident or at least easier to see. These are two very extreme but true scenarios. On paper, you may have a difficult time differentiating the assessment results of a socially accepted, well-behaved genius and a true psychopath. The same level of genius necessary to cheat, charm, and con others is necessary of some of the top CEOs, police officers, real-estate brokers, and even the annoying car salesman and the telemarketer you just hung up on. The trick is being able to balance the good and evil we all possess in a healthy way.

It's crazy to admit it sometimes, but I can see where my kind of crazy came from. For many years logic and practicality were easily replaced by anger and resentment. Each criticism, insult, and pain brought on by people closest to me tore at me like the strike of a hammer, the tools of a sculptor. I sometimes feel like I've been slowly but skillfully shaped into an educated monster born in the East, raised by marines, and molded in the West by liars, thieves, and intellectuals alike. Here at work, among people who have committed some of the most unthinkable crimes, I am truly invisible, as most of my colleagues are. It's here that my kind of crazy is easily overlooked.

I often wonder how it is that I can sometimes guess exactly what it is my patients are thinking without them even saying a word. I've been called psychic before. I've surprised myself more than I thought I could. I've even considered that I might be good at what I do because I think just like them. Does this make me crazy? Holy shit!

There are times when I've stood in front of an angry patient and gone toe to toe with him, hoping that I'm right in the assumption that he won't do anything to hurt me. Trust me when I say the last thing I want is to be punched, spit on, or knocked down, but when this doesn't happen I am more and more convinced that my patients believe I am much more aligned with them than I should be. I feel like one of those characters in a zombie movie who gets passed by because I smell just as bad as the zombie I've befriended and have been hiding under my bed.

At what point does the line get crossed? I've never done anything unethical or that actually crosses any lines... unless you hold it against me that I told a patient once I didn't think his suicide plan was good enough. Or that I later blew him off and never completed my therapy session with him. I was still a student though. I've come a long way since then. Either way, we all know that perception means more than anything more often than not. Just doing the right thing sometimes puts me at odds with my colleagues. Advocating for not only what I believe in but for what is right has placed me in pretty difficult positions on more than one occasion.

I can't stand anything intolerant and unjust. Maybe being treated unfairly in the past was preparation for what I do today. Maybe I had to know what it felt like to be hurt, treated badly, discriminated against and misunderstood in order to truly grasp the importance and seriousness of my work. Can just being myself be both my greatest ability and downfall? I mean, what good is anything if there is nothing on the line? If there is no fear and nothing to lose, then what are any of us fighting for? If I am not afraid everyday of losing everything I've gambled to be here, then what am I doing, and what else could there possibly be that could drive me? More important, what are these places I work at here for? Why do they exist if the people trained to work in them don't truly believe they can make a difference? Aren't I supposed to fight for myself? Aren't I supposed to fight for others?

The prisoners I worked with always told me I was not like any of the other therapists. "Yo, you cool as hell. You remind me of my girl back on the streets." Well, if we are truly the company we keep, then I don't think that's a compliment, and if it is, I should probably be afraid of myself— afraid of what I'm capable of and who I have the potential of becoming.

I can't fix everything and everyone. The expectation I've placed on myself to do this keeps me locked in this cycle that does nothing but hold me back and feed my anger and resentment. I keep repeating the same story over and over again, and it always ends the same. Someone pulls me in, I get stuck trying to pull us both out. I lose a piece of myself when I can't. I need to do something different. I can't continue to be so drawn in that I become part of the problem instead of the solution. I need to accept that it is not my job to bear the burdens of everyone around me. Half of me does not belong to everyone else. I am whole, and I am much stronger than I have ever been.

My story is supposed to be about experience and growth, not about how I cycle and repeat. I didn't hang my brother. If my sister dies, it will not be by my hands or lack of effort to save her. I can't save all my patients. They don't all want to be saved. How the people closest to me choose to live their lives, how my patients choose to live their lives—it has nothing to do with me. It's hard to say this, even harder to accept it, but not accepting it is making me obsessive and crazy. I am slowly going insane.

I will always wonder what I could have said or done differently at home and at work. The new me that I want to be, however, knows that at the end of the day, not only can I not save the world, but that the world is not mine to save. I must learn to live with this. I must learn to not be so angry. I must learn to live with my grief. Or I can continue to be too involved, not let go when I should, not walk away when all signs say it's time. But then nothing will ever change. I need to get my head on straight and stop this cycle I've created for myself. I'm better than this.

There she goes again. It's a fly she's chasing today. She's been at it most of the morning, stopping to nap for a few and then at it again. I look at her with admiration. It's not her father I see today—it's me. She's persistent. Like me, she's no quitter. She is focused. She is determined, very determined. Instead of telling her to go sit down somewhere before she breaks something jumping around the way she is, I watch her intently, hesitating only for a few seconds before I grab my flyswatter and join in. I know we'll probably never catch this damn fly, but sometimes doing the same thing over and over again helps bring some equilibrium and purpose to the world, to my life.

After a while we always figure it out. We all get to that aha moment eventually; we just need time. We also all need a little crazy to help push us along. That's how we survive. So if running around in my apartment with my dog chasing a fly gives her some purpose, then it's my job to support her. That is, until she realizes on her own that she may never catch this damn fly—or maybe she will.

Faith

I'm staring out of my office window at an empty street. I walk to the back doors leading to the enclosed backyard, and there is no one there. My house is quiet. There is only the sound of my pond. I have money. Lots of it, or at least more than most of the people I am surrounded by and more than I've ever had in the past. I have nice things, lots of them. I should be happy, but I am alone. My phone hasn't rung all day. I have not crossed the mind of a single one of my friends. What good is anything when it's not enough to fill the hollow space created by heartbreak? I had everything my heart desired: a good job, a successful business, great friends, a house in my name, and money in the bank. But I was sad and didn't have a clue how I was going to make it through the next thirty minutes, let alone another day. There was no tangible item of any monetary value that could pull me out of that.

My family has long since forgotten about me. When the yeses slowly became no's, and the money stopped flowing as easily as it once had, it became easier to forget and harder to pretend. I am not lonely. I like the silence. I like the peace. I like the absence of people asking things of me I don't want to give or do. I don't like the person I was forced to be, always smiling even when my heart ached. When I miss others, family and friends, it is the place they once filled and not the people they are that I mourn. Some days I awake fearing tomorrow more than death itself. Otherdays? When you think you're already dead, there is no reason to be afraid at all.

It's my first family therapy session, and I'm terrified. I was supposed to be meeting with a seventeen-year-old high school student who was court-ordered into therapy for excessive truancies, one of the many consequences she got slammed with for ditching too many times.

When the administrative assistant informed me that the entire family was in the lobby and planning to participate in treatment, I could have shit myself. I felt my heart rate pick up and fear instantly set in.

The family has been ushered back to the tiny room I'm sitting in. As soon as I close the door, I feel trapped. Mom is clearly devastated, at her wits' end, and ready to cry before her butt even hits the seat. I can't help but notice how quickly the temperature has just risen. I suddenly can't stop thinking about how much hotter this room is, and I'm feeling asthmatic. I'm also feeling panicky because the sight of people crying makes me super nervous and often leads to uncontrollable giggling or full-on laughter. When I am extremely nervous, I smile uncontrollably as well. I'm not sure which effect Mom will have on me, but neither would be appropriate or good.

I don't want to laugh, but Mom is falling apart already, so I smile at her to relieve the tension in my face and throat. I also deliberately minimize eye contact with her until the need to break into nervous laughter has completely subsided. The look of hopelessness on her face tells me she's got nothing left. This is no laughing matter for her. She has no clue why her daughter isn't going to school or where she goes instead. She also doesn't know why her daughter refuses to follow the rules at home or why she appears to be so mad all the time.

Dad can't believe that he got dragged into this mess. He just got done working all day, is still wearing his work uniform because he didn't even have time to go home and rest before being brought here, and the last place he wants to be is in this tiny-ass room that I reserved when I was expecting just one angry teenager. Now, like me, he's trapped. He's got it worse than I do, though. His wife is sad, his daughter is clearly pissed off, and I'm a ball of nerves. He's stuck in a room with three very emotional women. The look on his face is saying that he could use a drink. To be honest, I'm feeling like we could all use a drink, even the seventeen-year-old.

Upon meeting the family initial reaction was to refer out. There had to be someone who needed family therapy hours. I don't do families! The thought of sitting in a room with my own family was terrifying. We would never be able to focus on any one common goal without everyone at some point being the victim, having their feelings hurt, or walking out. Just thinking about it made my head hurt. I lost my faith a long time ago. Not just spiritually, but professionally. My unresolved resentment towards God had destroyed my faith in just about everything and everyone and was now impacted my ability to trust the skills I've learned to counsel this family effectively.

Reverend Wiley was more than the family pastor. And when I say family, I mean family. My cousins, aunts—all of us went to his church. His family was always there as well. I respected him, and I trusted him. So when my brother died, I went to him. I asked him why. If God sees everything and knows everything, how could he let this happen? Why weren't we warned? Why weren't we given the power to save him? Why hadn't he answered our prayers? Reverend Wiley spoke to me about free will, how God didn't choose this for my brother or us, how I had to move on. But how could I?

I'm only Christian because my parents were Christian. And truth be told, I'm only Christian when I'm not Catholic. Mom always kept us in church. If she couldn't go, or the car was broken down, which was often, mostly because we didn't have gas money, we would walk to the church nearest our home. When we were younger, we went to a Catholic church with our grandparents. If I had my choice at this age, I'd totally be Catholic. Not because I understood or believed anything that was said in that church, but because Catholics are fast. We stand, we kneel, we stand again, do some kind of modernized gang sign, swiping our hand across our chest and face, and we're done. The only thing that I found disturbing was that during communion we all had to drink from the same cup. There was nothing grosser than this at my young elementary school age. But it beat first, second, and on rare occasions third service, all-day choir rehearsals, and fighting to stay awake so that I didn't get pinched in the arm or popped in the back of the head by my mother during sermons that lasted for hours. This only after announcements have been read, introductions have been given, guests have been recognized, the choir has sung two to three extended versions of some well-known song by a crossover artist like Mary-Mary or Kirk Franklin, which don't get me wrong is always the best part, someone has caught the Holy Ghost, which will undoubtedly trigger another song by the choir or band, and everything else that precedes the minister speaking.

We really couldn't be sure that every time we prayed, we were praying to the right God. I made sure to mention that, had my parents been Muslim, I would be Muslim. And had my parents been atheist, I'd be atheist. My brother's death made me question my religion for the first time ever. There was no way in my young mind that a god, an all-powerful, all-knowing god, could allow this to happen. Reverend Wiley, the only human being I knew who could probably convince me that he too could walk on water and always had all the answers, simply looked at me and said "Faith."

"So why are you guys here?" I ask. I'm trying to sound friendly, matter-of-fact, and sincere. The truth is I am anything but. I have positioned myself directly in front of the one door that leads in and out of this room and am facing the clock, which is to everyone else's back or side. Having the door in direct sight helps me feel less trapped, and being able to see the time allows me to slowly watch the clock wind down. It wouldn't matter if someone came in with an instruction manual; at this point I have no idea how I am going to fill the next fifty minutes or so. All I can think about is how screwed up my own family is and how I am the last person anyone should be speaking to about family matters. I should be disqualified from family therapy based on my home life alone. We haven't even started, and I feel like a hypocrite.

"I'm here because she made me come," Dad says, quickly followed by, "I just want to go have a drink." *I hear ya, buddy—you and me both,* I think. He hasn't said much, but Dad is clearly my kind of guy. He says what he thinks. This will be useful. Mom doesn't respond verbally, but her nonverbal communication just about says it all. Her eyes are once again welling up as she shakes her head in disbelief at her husband's comment. Their daughter, Ms. "I'm not saying anything, and you can't make me," is sitting with her arms crossed, staring straight ahead, avoiding eye contact with anything that moves. I'm annoyed by her already, and Mom is just too damn emotional for me. I've decided that, in order to make it through the next eight to twelve weeks, I am soooo going to be Team Dad.

Faith? I'm a bit irritated that this is all he has to offer me. Clearly if I had faith, I wouldn't be here asking him about it. Although I hated long sermons and spending all day in church, my religious beliefs ran through my blood. It was as much a part of me as the skin on my bones. Everything I did centered on being a good Christian. I even sang in the church choir.

Our choir was hood, in a fun way. We were like a gang. Not just anyone could be in it. We had colors, songs, dance moves, and even hand signals. Our choir director told us when to rock and clap, when to sing softly, and when to turn it up. Within the walls of my church, we had our own gangsta glee club. Church had always provided a safe haven, a place of solace. I could talk to God, pray for the things I wanted and needed. I could practice my mad singing skills in front of a real audience. I had my own fan club. People would shout, dance, catch the Holy Ghost, and wave handkerchiefs and fans with random advertisements that had nothing to do with our church on them—all at the sound of my voice.

As a child I was no idiot. I knew what a miracle was; I'd seen it several times over. Bills got paid when we had no money to pay them. Tampons and toilet paper seemingly fell out of thin air. School supplies and clothes that I knew we couldn't afford showed up just in time. God was always talking to me. Sometimes his timing was a bit questionable, but he was there nonetheless. I could always count on him to show his hand when it was needed the most. When I was a child, God never disappointed. There was no such thing. The idea that a being so great and so indescribable could fail me was unfathomable. He could have done a better job at picking a father for me, but I had forgiven him for this many times over. He made up for it in boundless ways.

I think back over the things I've asked for: Christmas gifts, a record deal, to see my mom happy again. He had always come through in the past, but he was failing miserably in the present. Lately, God just couldn't find the time for me. I claimed to be atheist for several years because of this. You ignore me, I'll ignore you. Two can play that game.

I was much older now. Santa Claus and religion were about as real as fairies, mermaids, and vampires. I was in for the fight of my life. Have you ever picked a fight with god? As much I want to believe he doesn't exist, I'm too afraid to accept that this is true. Every day I awoke thankful that I was still breathing and given one more day to find the strength to reconcile. I mean, if he really does exist, he is the last person I'd want to piss off. The fear I live with every time I'm in my car? At work? It's like walking through life on eggshells. I was walking around each day wondering if this was the day I'd be condemned to an eternal hell. Oddly, the more afraid I became of not believing, the angrier I got, and the faster I lost my faith.

I never would have thought that religion, my relationship with God, would be one of the most prominent struggles in life. His invisibility, lack of physical presence, and the silence of his voice in my darkest hours—these are the hardest tests of faith that I have ever endured. And it takes all of me to muster the strength and courage necessary to win this fight. It's too hard for me, so I concede. With everything else I have to deal with, this is just something I am not ready to face. I truly believe that I may never win this fight. And with that, this chapter of my life, like my bible, the one I've carried with me since it was given to me after completing a book report on what I still believe is one of the greatest stories ever written, is indefinitely closed. I have other battles to fight today.

It has only been seven minutes. Time has somehow been able to rewind itself, and fear has set in. I want to call for my supervisor and lie, say I don't feel well, and I need to go home. The truth is that I don't feel well. But it's because I am terrified that I may do more harm than good here. In this moment I cannot separate my own personal problems from this family.

I grew up believing that the family as a unit was the most important thing in the universe and that I could do anything because I had my family's support. My values, my belief system, my morals are all built on the foundation of family. Yet I have no connection to them anymore. Who I am has always been associated with my role within my family. Without them, I don't know who I am some days. Was this some kind of test? Was I being challenged? Was this family sent to me in order to prove how important family is? No matter how bad things get, we should always make every effort to hold the family together?

I let my thoughts about my own family consume me, and what I am stuck contemplating is my own role; my own stubbornness. I realize that my family will never be fixed because we don't want to talk to one another. We don't know how. How anything will ever be resolved when no one is willing to talk is the problem, so that's what I focus on. I take a long, deep breath. I let it out. And I begin.

Over the next hour or so—yes, we went over the allotted fifty minutes—I get them to talk to one another, and I get them to listen. Even better, I teach them how to talk to one another, and I teach them the art of active listening and appropriate ways of responding. We even role-played. Even little Miss "I ain't saying shit" gets in on the act, and Mom stops crying long enough to process what's going on in this moment versus earlier in the day and all the days before.

I send them home that day with the first of many assignments: to write letters to one another, three letters each. Mom has to write to her daughter, her husband, and also to herself. These letters are to address her role, her promise of how she plans to change in order to help mend her family. Each letter has to be specific, including I statements, a discussion about their individual thoughts and feelings, and the impact this crack in their family was having on them.

Things turned out really well after twelve weeks. Mom and Dad went into an additional eight weeks of couples therapy to learn how to be a better team for their children. Their angry daughter actually grew a smile and went back to school. And I wrote a new curriculum for a new drug and alcohol treatment group that made it a requirement for the entire family to attend. When I was done training at this particular site, I stayed on as a volunteer for an additional six months for free. Family therapy didn't turn out to be that bad, after all. Once I trusted the process and my supervisor and considered everything I had been taught, it was actually fun.

I'm Okay!

A box showed up at my front door. It was marked *Vonage*. After I opened it and realized that it was the new router and phone connectors, I freaked out. Where the hell is the technician? How the hell am I supposed to figure this crap out by myself? I had been with my ex for ten years. There wasn't too much that he was good for, but hooking things up was on the list. I sit in the office chair in the back of my house staring at the box and the instructions. I've never liked reading instructions. If it doesn't come naturally to me, then I take it as a sign that I am not supposed to be doing it. I take the device out of the box, place it on the desk, and stare at it. I stare at it initially as if it will set itself up. I stare at it even longer because now I am irritated that at this point in my life, a time when I should be planning for my internship, a family, and a new career, I am instead going through a divorce. This may seem ironic. Although I never saw myself getting married, once I was, I never saw myself getting divorced. I never believed in divorce. I still don't. I always thought that as long as divorce was on the table as an option, people would take it over working through their problems. What I learned is that there are some problems that just can't be worked through.

I had a fairly decent high school experience. I thought I was going to be a writer, maybe even a television news anchor, so I wrote for the school paper, was on the yearbook committee, and participated in the morning news broadcast a few times a week. School was fun and I participated in a lot of functions and had a reasonable amount of friends. I especially loved my cohort. We were all close. We worked together, played together, and dated one another. We were in the air force ROTC program—future pilots, air traffic controllers, and officers. When I was selected to attend a trip to the air force academy in Colorado Springs, I had all but signed the contracts and was prepared to graduate, go off to boot camp, and start my life as a soldier. This is where things take a turn.

I had my entire life planned out. Plan A and a backup plan: if I couldn't be the next Brandy or Monica, I'd just be an officer in the air force. All I remember from my trip is that it was cold, and there was nothing to do out there in Colorado. To be bored and cold for the next four years of my life did not seem appealing to me at all.

What I remember most, however, was that part of successfully passing my courses at the academy included landing a glider, a tiny plane with no engine pulled into the air by a more realistic, completely functional airplane that actually has an engine. After you reach an altitude high enough to successfully plummet to your death, a string connecting you to the functional airplane ahead of you is released. You are then left to float your way back down to earth on your own. Although this seemed like a cool idea for most of my classmates, the idea that I was going to deliberately climb into a plane that has no engine, knowingly allow someone to pull me up to a height just high enough for me to hit the ground hard enough to splatter into pieces should I not make my landing, and then release me so that this unimaginable death, which I can totally imagine, becomes more likely, is way beyond my comprehension. The day I returned home, after four years of being groomed for the air force, I joined the Marine Corps.

I noticed the recruiter walking down the hallway of my school. His uniform was the most attractive military outfit I had ever seen in my life. After chasing down and speaking to him, I was in awe. Some may have been scared off by the number of weeks one would have to be away from family and friends and the intensity of the training itself, but me? If I was going to do this military thing, I might as well go into the toughest branch. I'd choose being gassed, pushed from a rappel tower, and fighting to survive after jumping from a diving board into the deep end of a pool with full pack and rifle, even though I am terrified of both heights and deep water, any day over smashing into the ground in an engineless death trap.

The reality is that I needed a way out and a way in. I needed a change. I didn't want to be poor anymore. I didn't want to be a manager at McDonald's or some other random fast food restaurant. I didn't want to stay on the east coast. I wanted to go to college. I wanted to travel. I wanted to be someone that I could look in the mirror and be proud of. The Marine Corps gave me a way out of a life of asking neighbors for eggs and sugar by giving me a salary, paying me to travel, and sending me to school. It gave me a way into a life that I had never known existed, a life that had never been modeled for me, and a way to branch out on my own to find what up to this point I never had—my own identity.

My whole life had been planned up to this point. But since my brother's death, I hadn't found the same enjoyment in music. I had been wavering on being a professional singer. My goals and ambitions drastically changed. For a long time, I tried to figure out where I belonged and which way I was to go after we buried him. I was treading in new territory. Being like Brandy and Ray-J, famous brother and sister, was no longer an option. I also had a taste of what it would be like to have my personal life plastered all over the front pages, and I didn't like it. After my brother's death, everyone had a comment or question. When? How? Why? I just wanted to grieve on my own, deal with his passing in my own way, in my own time. Instead I was too busy correcting the inaccurate rumors and fending off the questions and stares.

People wondered how bad it must have been growing up in my home for my brother to want to hang himself. I was asked that once. "Damn, what did your mom do to make your brother want to hang himself?" Why someone would think that this is an appropriate question to ask a child, especially about her mother, who was still grieving, stupefies me. More and more after his death, I found myself searching for answers and looking for something. I wouldn't know what it was for many years, but the more decisions I made that I wouldn't normally have made pre-funeral, the more at ease I became. So when I was told that I was too young to join the military, I convinced the recruiter to come to my home and talk my mom into signing me over. It took some persuading and a lot of threats from my mom to the recruiter, but she signed me over like a piece of property and that was that. I was off to boot camp, property of the United States Marine Corps three days after I graduated from high school.

I made a good life for myself. The military helped afford me the education I was looking for. I received a degree in communications, and although I double majored, studying molecular biology for two years, I quickly realized that I don't like blood. Actually, I don't like any bodily fluids at all. So, although initially I thought that if I couldn't get a job that allowed me to write for a living, maybe I would be a medical doctor of some kind, this idea quickly faded, and two years in I dropped biology. Medical school would no longer be an option.

The funny thing is that I realized I didn't have to touch people, at least not physically, to help them. And although I had originally signed up for a master's degree in American literature, I very quickly decided that psychology was more to my liking.

I love psychology! I found a home there. I feel like I've fallen into myself in this field. I understand more. I listen more. I speak more. Although I used to sit in silence and allow people to speak for me and about me, I now stood up for myself. I understood personalities, and I learned how to respond to them. Working in this field came easy—well, most of it came easy. Although I found it extremely easy to build rapport with most of my clients, there were some clients who just bored the hell out of me or made me feel as if I was doing more work than they were. *You're the one with the problem,* I would think. *Why the hell am I working so hard?* That was what bugged me about super-depressed clients. I spent a year and a half working with teenagers, and I loved it. Go figure—who would have thunk it? Me and teenagers in the same room actually getting along, and me actually wanting to be there? I shocked myself with this one.

Something I learned in my short time working as a counselor, therapist, and rehabilitation coordinator was how to communicate. I never realized just how hard it could be to sit and listen. To actively listen is really a challenge. Instead of paying attention, I myself have been guilty of waiting for that pause that lets me know it's okay to jump in and say my spill. How can I be listening if I'm planning my rebuttal?

To find that I, who could sit and talk to strangers and classmates for hours on end and have a decent, nonconfrontational conversation and yet go home and not say a word to my own husband for days on end was confusing and stressful. I was teaching a twelve-week course that centered on knowing how to effectively communicate, and I couldn't do it myself. I tried really hard to use the tools I had learned and was teaching, but somehow they just didn't work the same for me.

I felt so empowered at work. I was making a difference; a visible change in people's lives. My clients were happier, communicating better, getting along better, and making positive changes and decisions in their lives. At home, my own husband made me feel so inadequate. I was a superhero in the streets and at work and a disobedient, errant, nuisance in my own house. This reality of my conflicting worlds ate at me.

In recent years my husband insisted that I had changed, that I was somehow different. I now realize that I did change. While he was the same person he was the day I met him, married him, and threw in the towel, I had grown up. I wanted more for myself. I wasn't the same twenty-something, passive, it's okay, let-me-do-that-for-you kind of girl. If growing up and wanting more out of life than to just exist in the presence of someone else is changing for the worse, then I'm guilty. Somehow I still felt as if I would never be okay if I walked away. Filing for divorce was against everything I believed in.

So here I am, staring this Vonage device down. I'm trying to convince myself that I don't need a home phone. I start to just leave the device sitting there, hoping that someone, most likely my personal assistant, will stumble across it and set it up for me. As I head for the door, I stop. I'm not really sure why, but I turn around and immediately think, *How hard can this be?*

Twenty minutes later, without having read the instructions, because I'm willing to give this a try and set it up for myself but I'm still the same stubborn person I was an hour ago, I'm finished. I hesitate to pick up the phone receiver. I need to see if there is a dial tone to confirm my success, but I hate failure. I'm way more competitive than anyone should be, and not hearing that dial tone would just confirm that I need someone else to help me. I'm not good enough on my own. I will always have to depend on someone else. The ink hasn't even dried on my divorce papers. Even though I asked for this, I am still wondering if I did enough, if I gave enough, and what my role in this epic failure is.

For some reason hearing the dial tone and being able to make a call means so much more than just being able to set up some stupid little device. It was my way of proving to myself that I would be okay. My solace and peace of mind depend on what happens in the next few moments. I slowly lift the receiver and put it to my ear. I fall backward into the chair, still holding the phone to my ear, and start laughing. In this moment you can say whatever you want to me. You can call me whatever you want, even if it's out of my name and derogatory. The sky could fall on me right now, and it wouldn't bother me at all. As I listen to the dial tone, I somehow know that not only have I made the right decision in filing for divorce, but in this moment and from now on I am okay.

Epilogue

Denial and isolation were easy. I was already invisible. Pretending everything was okay was simple. There was always someone and something more important than me. I used work to mask my true pain. Work is the easiest excuse for being too busy to accept what has become my truth. Anger and bargaining, however, were the most natural. After begging God to intervene and promising to be a better sister and person and getting nothing in return, I put very little effort into sabotaging what remained of my life. I hated everyone.

For years all I could think about was what I did wrong. Why I didn't go up the stairs a few minutes sooner. What I could have been doing that was so much more important. How it was that I was peeling potatoes while he was dying. I wondered if I'd counted too high or too low and if each breath pushed into his body went into his lungs or stomach. I also wondered whether any of this would have even made a difference. I wondered if I could have been a better person. If being closer to him would have changed the outcome of that night. If me not being wrapped up in speech competitions, talent shows, and dance recitals would have changed the course that evening set us on.

Depression was my favorite. I was there for a long time. I still am sometimes. I often find myself wandering around aimlessly, wondering what my purpose is and what my life post-twin, post-music, post-military, and everything else I gave up on is supposed to be. When I think back on the most difficult times, I find my distress has presented in very unhealthy ways. This hasn't changed. Presently, when I'm struggling, I tend to revert to unhealthy eating patterns, for example. My sudden drop in weight often gives me away. On nights when I couldn't sleep, I resorted to alcohol and Nyquil, but only on the most difficult nights because I was afraid of becoming addicted. There is a sense of hopelessness because it's during these periods that I realized I could die at any moment without warning, and that scared me. Even though it made no sense, in my mind there was always this increase in risk of wrecking my car, getting fatally injured at work, or becoming the victim of some random street crime. This only made things worse. As my depression increased, so did my anxiety and anger. Being angry takes allot of work. It's an exhausting way to live.

What I have learned over the years, however, is that I don't need anyone's approval. My grief has changed me for the good. Of course, there are some things I continue to work through and days I don't have the energy to get out of bed, but I think this is to be expected considering I lived this way, grieving, for so long. I also realized I don't need as many people in my life as I once thought I did. For a very long time, I sought support, approval, and validation from people I didn't even like. For whatever reason, no matter how much I disliked them and how unhealthy a role they played in my life, what they thought mattered. Every decision I made for a long time was based on what I thought others would say and do in response. The moment I realized I didn't need what I'd been fighting so hard for all this time, I was able to move into acceptance.

Acceptance is not all-encompassing. Bad days send me backpedaling toward depression.

Ever since my first episode, I've noticed it has become easier and easier to send me back to that place. The smallest things tend to set me off as I typically internalize external matters. Even so, there are some aspects of life and death that I've learned to just take as they are, as they were. I can't change the fact that death occurred, for example. That is not the part I struggle with. It's the how and when that I beat myself up about. I accept that he is gone. I don't accept that there was nothing I could have done that would have made some difference. What that difference would have been, I don't know, but I can't imagine that if the five of us who were in that house that night had been in different places, doing different things, the result would have been the same. But I didn't put that belt around his neck. I didn't not try to save him. I'm not a bad person or a failure because I failed him even because I couldn't save him.

People tend to think of psychologists as well put together and all-knowing. We tend to think we can fix everyone's problems. Maybe it's the truth in our own lives that make us the most relatable, compassionate, and understanding. Maybe, although no one wants to admit their therapist used to be an alcoholic, is mentally ill, or in therapy themselves, these are the things that validate the services we provide and make us better at providing them.

There are a lot of things people can find fault with in me, things others may never accept. But I'm happy with who I am today. When presented with the other options, I hope I'll always choose to be happy. It's the thing I've worked the hardest for in my life. There is no amount of money, objective, or person that can replace the joy I feel when I truly take inventory of who I am and how far I've come. I am not perfect and will never be. And I'll probably always struggle at my attempts to settle my soul. There is a void that remains, and I am reminded of that void allot when I'm at work, but these reminders are far less frequent than they used to be.

Who I am is in part largely about being able to acknowledge and accept even the most hidden parts of me. These include the parts I am afraid others won't like but am no longer afraid to share. Always having secrets and baggage and trying to hide who I really am from others takes too much time and effort. I can't do it anymore. I don't want to do it anymore. It's not important that you accept who I am, but it is important when interacting with me that you know who I am. I am always anxious. I'm afraid to fail but equally as afraid to succeed. Success in my life has not always been met with positive rewards. I am also afraid of being hurt by others, including patients, family, and friends I may let get too close. Because of this I go to great lengths to keep distance between myself and others. I may always be this way. I may never let you in or allow you to get close to me.

I am afraid to be in control but more afraid of giving up control. No one will fight for me as hard as I will. No one will protect me as fiercely as I will. I know this to be true. So I am controlling. I am emotionally disconnected and socially inept at times. I will always attempt to sit in the same seat or stand in the same corner when I enter a room. I will almost always shy away from crowds because I am terrified to be among groups of people. This is especially the case when I don't know anyone else in the room. I have had more panic attacks than I'd like to admit. Because of this I almost never go out alone, avoid supermarkets whenever I can, as well as most other stores, malls, get-togethers—that is, unless someone I know is with me, although sometimes even this isn't enough.

I am humble and often embarrassed about receiving positive feedback and accolades, especially in the presence of others, even if I deserve it. I can be arrogant and stubborn. The latter, however, tends to serve mainly as a form of defense when I feel threatened. Although I am not dumb, I often believe I am the least intelligent person in the room. I can be insecure because I always tend to focus on all the things I am lacking instead of all the gifts I have been given.

I remember my failures, like that patient I couldn't convince to not commit suicide, but not the ones I've helped save. I will always remember those lost because they are the ones that drive me to be better and to work harder. I am confident but only when not comparing myself or being compared to others. I am often too serious, but this is caused by a life of constant fighting and always having my guard up.

I am an introvert. I may lie to get out of social activities and events. It is not personal, but yes, though you may find it hard to believe, I'd much rather be at home alone in a candlelit room with a glass of wine, curled up with a book or spinning records, than at a party turning it up with you.

I have some obsessive and compulsive behaviors and am a bit of a germaphobe. If you look closely, you may see a ritual or two or three. I won't shake your hand because I don't know where it's been, and I'm afraid of your germs. This may lead me to wear my gloves indoors, even when it's hot as hell, in order to avoid skin-to-skin contact.

Some say that I am extremely picky, but my therapist says I am just particular. I believe her because, by accepting money from me, she has silently agreed to always tell me what I want to hear, even though she doesn't know this. Because I pay her, however, I will also never completely trust her or believe what she says to be true unless it benefits me or she no longer stands to benefit financially from my continued attendance.

I am funny as hell, or so I've been told, although I feel like people spend much more time laughing at me rather than with me. I am long-winded and will probably always give you the long version of stories and answers. This is for your benefit because I don't trust that if I give you the short version you will truly understand what I'm saying. The long version, even when redundant, ensures you will get it—at least that's what I tell myself.

I am abrupt and direct more often than not, and you may be offended by this, although hurting you is usually not my intent. When I don't care to be around you or am bored and don't feel like being bothered, I am moody and brash. I can be short-tempered. If I'm pissing you off however, it may be my deliberate attempt to get you to leave me alone. It's the quickest way to get you to give me some space. Although I could just say, "I need some space," that would make me look weak. So I have to be mean to you.

I think with my mouth open and sometimes speak too fast to catch the things that come out of it. I speak allot when I am nervous. I shut down completely when I am afraid. I am often indifferent about things I should be taking a stance on. I'm usually way too opinionated about things that have nothing to do with me. Although I am known to advocate or others, I sometimes struggle when it comes to speaking up for myself. This is especially so when I think it may lead to a confrontation. I am a busybody. I have racing thoughts, am more curious than I should be, and am always in search of answers, even when there are no clear answers to be found. I need to make sense of every person, place and thing that surrounds me. But I also need proof because, although you think I enjoy debating with you, the truth is that my mind won't let me settle for just your opinion. I am a scientist, so give me facts and support them.

I have been told by some that I can be cold and judgmental while others swear by my compassion, understanding, and generous spirit. I am a twin. I will always be a twin. I am hurting, and will probably always hurt. I am protective of my heart and the hearts that have been entrusted to me. I am loyal to a fault. Whether you know it or not, you want me on your team.

Change takes time. It doesn't happen because of what we say or do. Patients need to see and feel the humanity in us clinicians. They need to know we are not with them because we are checking a box or completing a task. They get their hope from us. We look them in the face and convince them we believe in them. We convince ourselves they can change. As officers do when they are attempting to pull a confession from a criminal, we break these guys down. We go at them with compassion, positive regard, and treatment that allows them to save face and reconcile who they are with who they want to become. It may take a while: weeks, months, years. But eventually they break—when they're tired of the walls, the chains, the monotone uniforms that scream "I'm a monster—watch out for me." When they reach the point when they no longer want to feel the way their existence behind, away and shut out from everything they desire and love makes them feel, we've got them. In the midst of their hopelessness comes their ability to compromise their flawed and distorted beliefs and morals, to be receptive, willing to do the work and eventually to change. It's the same for us—for me. Not too many people like being in that dark place for too long. Eventually, we look for ways out. Some of us make it.

Muhammad Ali once said that our service to others is the rent we pay for our space here on earth. I hold these words as close to my heart as my own belief in the good we all possess, and I'm partly driven by them. I enjoy helping others. My desire to see you become better gives me the fuel I need to make it through a ridiculously long and busy day. My patients are my CPR. My friends are my CPR. My newfound love for life itself is my CPR. Whether the air goes into my lungs or stomach doesn't matter—I am given life. One person at a time, I have become stronger than I was yesterday. I have learned that life gets better. And knowing what I know about how much better life can be empowers me to help others realize their potential even when they cannot yet see it.

Every day I work to prove my worth, my intelligence, and my right to everything life has given me. I remind myself that as much as I desire the validation and acceptance of my boss, my friends, my family, and colleagues, my own opinion of myself is equally as important, if not more. It is a daily task reminding myself that I am enough, just as I am.

The past few years have been extremely profitable in terms of growth, experience, and building worthwhile and meaningful relationships. I accept that there is power in my pain. I also accept that with vulnerability comes strength. I love what I do. I am learning to love the person I've become. I couldn't imagine life without the daily hustle of group therapy, individual therapy, and treatment planning. My work grounds me.

My flaws don't make me incompetent. My hurt doesn't make me an expert. My experiences, however, have made me a pretty amazing psychologist.

And now a sneak peek at *Special*.

By M.J. Rex

Special

By M. J. Rex

Prologue

I'm riding down the Avenal Cutoff at eighty miles per hour, leapfrogging my way home from work. Everyone is moving so slowly, but I'm in a rush as usual. I have no plans, but there is a sense of urgency for me to get as far away from this place as I can. I realize that I am no different than them. The patients and prisoners that roam the halls are all remnants of a past they no longer own. Their stories have been rewritten over and over again, and each time the story gets told, they become more and more monstrous. I don't want my story rewritten. I don't want it told at all.

It's dark, and I can see the lights of a truck approaching slowly. I wonder where it's going. I'd give anything to be able to pick up my things and just go, start over somewhere new. Reality has a funny way of reminding me that I have little control over my life. I don't like it. I notice my battery light come on. It's enough to send me over the edge. Calmly I lift my hands above my head and catch the air above my sunroof window as I speed away. With my hands no longer on the steering wheel, my car, as if it has a mind of its own, begins to turn. The lights on the truck are beautiful, and I am drawn to them like a bug to a flame. I close my eyes, take a deep breath, and I take it in…

Chapter One

I have checked my front door for what feels like the sixth or seventh time. I know I'm obsessing, but I can't stop. It began with the locks on the front door but soon evolved to patio doors, windows, and then the kitchen. I check to ensure I haven't left the stove on at least four times a night. I check each burner knob, open the oven door to feel for heat, and sometimes stand there for several minutes in search of what could be the smell of gas. I do this every night, even on nights I haven't used my stove, which are not so rare. I have woken up after only an hour or two of sleep and repeated my checks after scaring myself awake from the nightmares and constant worrying. Recently I've begun looking under my bed and behind both closed and open doors. I don't know what I'm looking for, but it's part of my nightly routine. Although it helps me to sleep better, it also keeps me up most nights.

I am lonely. Unable to sleep, I find myself standing in the dark living room in my expansive, open-layout sitting room. It overlooks the pier. From here I have one of the best views of Woodstock, especially at night. I've always been attracted to water. Although I fear it, I also respect it. We, the ocean and I, have somewhat of an unspoken romance. I sit with her every evening so that neither one of us is lonely, and she sings me to sleep on my most troubled nights. It's my dream home in my dream neighborhood. All of my neighbors are wealthy. We are the Who's Who of Petersburg County, the uppity part of Woodstock, Willingboro.

I am eventually greeted by my three-year-old dog, Hope. I love her to death and couldn't imagine life without her, but I don't touch her. I cannot bring myself to pet her fur. I am repulsed by her in so many ways. Even though we don't speak the same language, I am convinced that she understands me. And because she understands me, she forgives me for not loving her in the physical way I know she would like me to. She keeps me company on the worst nights, when thoughts of my past and patients and their well-being keep me awake. She runs with me further than I should be running as I barely eat on most days and am a too-thin 136 pounds. I know she is tired and hot. Her resting body temperature is a ridiculously warm 102 degrees. I feel awful sometimes, dragging her along on four-to six-mile jogs in eighty degrees of hell. When I need to clear my mind, however, this is the best remedy. The more stressed I am, the longer we run. Her presence creates the illusion of invisibility and safety. People who get too close often get a growl. She almost never barks, but when she does, it's clear she's not one to be tested. She can feel my discomfort when others get too close. She protects me the only way she knows how. And even though I often yearn for pillow talk on rainy nights, an embrace from someone strong when I am at my weakest, and, as she most likely does as well, the physical touch of another, I cannot be vulnerable, not even with her on most days, and she accepts this. She accepts me.

I cannot trust. I don't know how. I have major issues with commitment. I cannot and will not put someone else's needs before my own. Not in my personal life, at least. Not like I did in the past. I cannot open myself up to anyone besides this four-legged animal who is only allowed to hear my worst because she can't talk and therefore can't tell my secrets. Because of this, it wouldn't be fair to invite another into my home. Who in their right mind would be okay with just having pieces of me? And so I am often alone. It's my choice, but the consequences are not. They are simply my burden to bear by default and Hope's as well.

Chapter Two

"What the hell?!" It is way too early for this. I'm usually here by 8am, but another sleepless night has brought me in over an hour earlier than usual. It's 7am, and I can barely keep my eyes open. I leave my office to find someone I can bribe to do a Starbucks run. I enter the hall, where I am immediately bombarded by the sounds of what is sure to be World War III if I don't get there fast. As I turn the corner into the hall leading to the first-floor bathroom, I see patients and staff running around everywhere.

"I'm sorry, Doctor C—Jesus Number One just met Jesus Number Two," Dexter says as he runs by me. No matter how many times I remind staff that you cannot place two similarly diagnosed patients together, this continues to be an occasional occurrence. I'm beginning to believe the staff do this on purpose in order to see what will happen. It is my license that's on the line, however, and I don't find these random experiments funny at all. Although there are times when psychotic patients can coexist in small quarters such as the ones we have here, it only works when they don't believe they are the same person.

"Please get it straightened out," I say way too calmly as I head for my first individual therapy session of the day, giving up on my search for a coffee fairy.

Trust me, I'm a liar. That's what I'm thinking as she takes a seat in front of me. I usually don't lie to patients, but I also know that in this case I am willing to say whatever I need to in order to save her. Even if it's not 100% true. I am honestly unsure of my ability to save her. But when I tell her things can get better I need her to believe me. So I say it anyway. That's what I'm thinking as she takes a seat in front of me. She wants to die. I want to save her. I need to save her. She's only been here a little while, but it's clear she's different. She's not like the other ones who say they want to die but really just want some attention. Their screams at two in the morning, the blood smearing and cutting, that's their way of saying, help me. She, on the other hand, doesn't want my help. She's made this pretty clear. She doesn't want my attention. The second I turn my back, she'll do it.

"I like you, Dr. C. I respect you a lot. I can't promise you that I won't hurt myself, but I will promise that it won't be during your shift," she tells me. This is her promise to me. I want to say thank you. Part of me appreciates her desire to spare me the devastation of watching or hearing her die, or finding her body during my occasional room checks or staff's ten-minute rounds. Part of me wants to tell her to just do it already, just get it over with. I've grown tired of the daily routine of stalking her in order to ensure she is still alive. I've obsessed over her for far too long. She's been here for three weeks already and she is just as focused and determined today as she was the day she arrived. I try not to call her by name. I'm afraid to get to know her. I'm afraid of what her death will do to me. I've stood outside her room several times watching her chest rise and fall, and it's exhausting. This twenty-four-hour suicide watch is stressful and draining. Even when I'm not here at work, I'm thinking of her. I feel like she's holding me hostage by not just doing it already and instead dragging both of us through this horrendous process of waiting. I don't know what it's like to be her, to hear voices, to have people stare at me funny and treat me differently because of a disease I can't control. I can't and may never understand what it's like to look at my own children and fear that they will die by my hands. To lose control of myself and lose time and space and distance from people and things. To question reality and everything about it that makes me human. But I can relate to her sadness. And I want to save her. I need to save her.

I spend about an hour with her, with Dee-dee. Although I never call patients by their nicknames because it seems too personal, I've picked up the habit of referring to Dee-dee by hers. This is mainly because it helps to not feel as close to her. I convinced myself that not using her real name has in some ways made her less real, and should it come to it, less of a loss if she actually dies. She is still suicidal. We talk about her children and the impact her loss will have on them. She tells me about her experience of childrearing. Although I've never had any children, I am quite sure that describing this process as incubation is not how most mothers would remember it. She relates to everything and everyone in her life with such distance. It's no wonder she feels so disconnected. I give her an assignment that encourages her to write a what-if scenario. If her death had a negative impact on the lives of her children, what would this look like? I need her to envision the possibility of being missed and grieved and begin to reconnect to her family—to anyone.

It's a pretty quiet day. An uneventful day around here is rare. After finishing my last few individual therapy sessions and shift change, I head out a little early. I am still craving and in need of a pick-me-up. A quiet day at work usually meant an opportunity to pick at the stack of paperwork sitting in the corner of my desk. It was always needing attention and steadily growing in size. But I need to go before something does happen, which is usually the case when a day goes by as slowly as this one. Just as we all begin to say our good nights, someone starts screaming, someone goes off baseline, an argument breaks out—it's the end-of-the-day curse, and we've all grown to expect it, so quite often about thirty minutes before the day ends, people begin to slowly disappear. Patients knew it was shift change time, so they were typically enjoying the last bit of free time before mandatory evening treatment groups began.

Even though I left the facility early, I'm in a rush as I walk over to Starbucks, finally. I can't believe I've made it an entire day without an ounce of caffeine. Lord knows I'll need some for tonight. I guess I could have driven and left straight from Starbucks, but I needed the fresh air. Walking was sure to put me behind schedule and make me late, but the three-block stroll was something I often did to clear my head and compartmentalize work from home life. I'd agreed to attend a charity event with Cassidy this evening. I love her to death, but her energy was abnormally robust all the time. There's no way I'll survive several hours with her without a pick-me-up.

Cassidy and I have been friends for over ten years, and in that time she has never let me get away with standing her up, attempting to stand her up, or being late. So when I show up almost thirty minutes late even after having left the office thirty minutes early, I am actually dreading seeing her.

I don't even know how I let her talk me into this. Change for Change is an organization she has volunteered for as long as I've known her. Over the past three or four years, it has picked up attention for its college funds, which have sent close to twelve hundred children who grew up in shelters and low-income homes and communities to college, it was still a fairly small, up-and-coming organization that survived on small donations from mostly anonymous contributors such as myself. This meant we had to hit the pavement often. Cassidy has never been able to talk me into hosting an event for them before, but after losing a bet, here I was. Thankfully, the only thing hosting really included was showing up and footing the bill for the catering and supplies, which I was happy to do.

Cassidy greets me with a smile and hug. She doesn't even mention the fact that I just strolled in here late and with Starbucks, which is a huge no-no in her world. I can hear her saying, "If you had time to stop, then you had time to get here on time!" But there's nothing. She's got something up her sleeve. I hate surprises, and I know she's got one for me. I'm already regretting my decision to come.

About the Author

The assumption that I hear the most from patients about Psychologist is that they have chosen the field of Psychology because they too are looking for answers. Even so, for decades it has been taboo for Psychologist to openly reveal and discuss the very struggles patients are often referring to. Patients' tend to forget that Psychologists are human too. The expectation is that, in a field nurtured by selflessness, the patient always comes first. This, at times, comes at the expense of the clinician. M. J. Rex speaks about her journey towards a career as a Forensic Psychologist. Her unique perspective gives not only an inside look at how personal and professional life can become entwined, but how this process of entanglement actually helps to mold her into a more experienced and relatable clinician. Depressed People Make Me Sleepy also touches on the almost unspoken reality that there are mentally ill clinicians providing above average treatment. M. J. very openly talks about her grief and loss, depression, overwhelming anxiety, family discord, her relationship with food, anger, abuse, and her role as a female throughout her life and career. More importantly however, she manages to explain, sometimes in extremely vivid detail, how these tragedies became the foundation of her success and personal growth..

Made in the USA
Las Vegas, NV
17 December 2020